Automate or be Automated

By David Vivancos

To Everybody That Lost Someone
by The Covid-19 outbreak.

Contents

David Vivancos Cerezo

Science & Technology Serial Entrepreneur.

 With pioneering activities since 1995 in fields as Internet, Java, Electronic Art, Virtual Reality, Artificial Intelligence, Apps, Nano Sciences, 3D Printing, Neuro Computing or Deep Learning, including starting up 5 ventures and several initiatives in these fields.

Keynote Speaker and Author with more than 300 conferences, seminars and workshops lectured worldwide in Europe & US. Associate lecturer in several universities, business schools & corporations.

Advisor to boards & CEOs from Fortune500s to innovative startups in the journey from the digital world to the fully automated world.

Artificial Intelligence Algorithmist, with hundreds of thousands deep learning code lines developed.

Web: http://www.vivancos.com
Books: https://amazon.com/author/davidvivancos
Email: vivancos@vivancos.com
LinkedIn: http://www.linkedin.com/in/davidvivancos
Twitter: @VivancosDavid

Why I wrote this

We are living times of unprecedented change, and to be able to cope with it, we need to be part of the process, otherwise we will be left apart.

Being part of process means leading it to the best of our potentials, not just following the wave or even worst, just missing it, and believe it or not there are still opportunities to be part of the coming change.

The change I am referring is the automated world, driven by Artificial Intelligence and Robotics, that is starting to displace humans from the workforce, will redefine our societies, our lives and even our own human nature.

The change itself is not good or bad, it is simply a new era that is looming, far beyond what some people call the fourth industrial revolution. Since the implications span to facets of life never believed to be challenged previously through human history.

I explored some of these challenges in my previous book "From Big Data to Artificial Intelligence 2019 Edition", and this book will dive into how we can be part of this coming change, be prepared and act instead of being carried away by the wave of innovation and transformation.

For being part of it, we need to become teachers of machines, not only mere users, since in our human nature we still have lots of clues not yet mastered by machines, and due to our uniqueness we can all add key ingredients to the process, and in the meanwhile make our lives easier and more profitable.

It is the time to learn relentlessly about these topics, from the theoretical and practical stand points, it is also the time to create it together, stablish the frameworks and start the think tanks necessary so everyone is included, and nothing relevant is left to chance, not with fear but with the mindset of the explorer of a new frontier that we all must reach.

I wrote this book to share my 30+ years devoted to building science and technology endeavors, that converge now in a unique moment in our shared history, due to this new capabilities learned by machines almost taken from a science fiction movie script, but far from it, since this new reality is being created every day at a speed that surprise even us while we build it.

The book is on the making for several years, but before finishing it and publishing it, I needed to test first my assumptions, through real life lived experiences helping automate from startups to big corporations, so I could share real and practical wisdom, not only fiction scenarios that may or may not become true, it does not meant that you will not also find a few hints from my personal vision of the future.

I suggest you to read it with your mind open, beyond what you think is now possible, and more importantly try to test it for yourself, the book is just the beginning of what should be a lifelong learning initiative in this field, since all written words are history and this book is no exception.

David Vivancos
San Lorenzo de El Escorial
March 27th 2020

CHAPTER ONE:

Automate My Life

From human to automata?

As human beings we have develop and inherited incredible capabilities in many facets of our lives, some are closely linked to our physical and mental capacities and limitations, to overcome some of these limitations we have also developed technologies and tools.

As humans we start with a nice but fragile "hardware", by default, our body has several external moving parts like two arms, two legs and a head, if we haven't lost any of them or born so.

Each of them also has many other moving parts that shape most of our interactions with the world and its entities, like our feet and toes, hands and fingers and of course our senses, mostly in our head like vision, hearing, taste, smell, and touch that runs through all our bodies.

Basically, we have a plethora of "**actuators**", some of them can rotate, move or exert pressure and we also have "**sensors**", like our eyes or ears, and most of them attached through all our skin and beneath creating an incredible network to "feel".

We may take all this for granted, but when we take a closer look at them, we realize, that they are the first physical interaction point that we have.

Internally all this is ruled by many internal organs and systems that enable and control the moving parts.

Exploring these diverse interactions, like the ones that take place between parts of our own bodies, or others that link our body with the external world, we can appreciate that some operate with full autonomy, some with semi-autonomy and a few are directly "controlled" by "us".

On the "mental side" we also start with a great "software" to deal with the above, ruled also by a network of connected cells, mixing biology with electricity in a unique combination that produces what we usually call intelligence.

It is true that the knowledge of our bodies anatomy has been increased vastly over the last centuries, and to some extent we master some of it, mostly bellow our heads, but it will be presumptuous to think that we know how our brain and all its parts functions, in fact I think that the opposite is true, I have been privileged to work with brain signals since 1998, neuro-technologies has been my main activity for several years, and currently I work in the intersection between Neuroscience and Artificial Intelligence, so it is fair to say that it is part of my job to be up to date in this field.

Basically my view of the subject is that **we don't have yet the tools with enough resolution to measure and explore a living human brain in real time and in full detail**, and we also lack of the knowledge to understand at a deep level, how it works.

This is not a new field at all, over the last few millennia it has been the pursue of many great minds, like *Hippocrates*[2], *Plato*[3], *Leonardo Da Vinci*[4], *Piccolomini*[5], *Descartes*[6], *Thomas Willis*[7], *Raymond Vieussens*[8], *Humphrey Ridley*[9], *Paul Broca*[10], *Santiago Ramon y Cajal*[11], *Cecile Vogt*[12] or *Hans Berger*[13].

Or in the last decades fantastic scientists of our time like *Rafael Yuste*[14], *Jack Gallant*[15], *Antonio Damasio*[16], *Miguel Nicolelis*[17], *David Eagleman*[18], *Mary Lou Jepsen*[19] or *Adam Gazzally*[20], to name just a few.

Even all these incredible individuals that purse the edge of the field, have a limited understanding of it, and have spent innumerable hours of its precious time exploring the subject.

Limited but key, by any means we should diminish the relevance of the amazing discoveries so far made by them and we all should be thankful for the talented humans that made this possible.

It is worth mentioning a plethora of entrepreneurs and visionaries, that are helping move the field forward, taking the tools of neuroscience from the science realm & the labs to consumers. Like *Tan Lee*[21] with her pioneer EEG startup Emotiv Inc[22] with whom I was privileged to work, precisely in data science and Artificial Intelligence.

She summarizes brilliantly the state of the art of the discipline in her last 2020 book "The Neuro Generation", a must-read.

She is not alone in the field, other entrepreneurs are paving the way so Neuro-technologies someday will become mainstream, like *Stanley Yang*[23] @ NeuroSky Inc[24], or *Ariel Garten*[25] & *Derek Luke*[26] @ Interaxon Inc[27], or *Ramses Alcaide*[28] @ Neurable Inc[29], or getting a step beyond, and mixing brains & technology with implantable devices, entrepreneurs like *Bryan Johnson*[30] @ Kernel Inc[31], or even *Elon Musk*[32] with NeuraLink[33], to name just a few.

It is relevant, to point out, that regardless of the incredible efforts, the truth is that we know very, very, little of how our brain works, not because we have moved in the wrong direction, mostly because we don't have yet the enabling technologies and probably a better theory to understand it so we can move forward much faster.

Our brain weights about 3 to 4 pounds, it consumes about 20 to 25 wats of the 100 wats that the full body is thought to consume, it can work without replacements for about 100 years and it contains about **100 billons neurons with trillions of connections**, probably in constant neuro-genesis with about **1500 new neurons generated every day**, to name a few facts.

There are three main types of neurons, **"Sensory Neurons"** dealing with the external stimuli captured by our senses, **"Motor Neurons"** handling the whereabouts of our muscles and **"Interneurons"** connecting the other two types. It is thought that there are about 10,000 different subtypes of these three.

Our brain it is without doubt the most complex device we know of, but nevertheless using a few "simple" components.

But why I am going through the nuts and bolts of our physiology? because they are the building blocks that shape our capacities and draw our limitations.

And these capacities allow us to have a working life on our daily basis. What we can or can't do is initially limited by that, influences the time it takes to perform each action we perform, physical or not, and shapes the boundaries we are born with, or have a given point in our lifetimes. Some of them we can stretch through training and maybe a few of its limits are probably still to be fixed, since human performance and endurance never ends surprising us, for example we see it every time an athlete breaks a record.

Reducing ourselves to moving parts and a "controller", may seem like a mechanistic approach, probably even from another age in time, but bear with me, we need to go to the basics, since it the best way to tackle something as big as complex as human behavior could be.

Yes, human behavior because at the end, **when we want, or need to automate ourselves, we need to either automate the end results of our actions or the actions themselves**, and for that we need to review the mechanics of it.

It is also true that the deeper you want to go, it gets more complex, using our intuition it should be the other way around, since we are trying to understand the underling nature of the subject, for example an atom is "simpler" than a planet, the problem comes when you don't have tools to work at a given scale, and the number of interactions grows exponentially.

Looks like every time we try to understand more about something, new doors open, and new avenues of knowledge keep us in a never-ending loop of seeking to understand it all. Something probably out of our reach, at least at each given point in time, but may seem feasible when we look back in time, the problem is that we will be cheating, since at the time we are looking at, we did not have the tools and the knowledge we have now.

I always say that you connect the dots afterwards, and the sooner you connect them the better off you end. Also, the finer or the higher resolution of the dots also influences the outcomes, as long as we have the tools to make and understand its connections.

Our range of actions is also influenced by the **tools** we create, and the ones that we learn how to use, since they extend our "built in" capabilities, and there are a wide range of them, some almost prehistoric, and some from literally yesterday, from tools to cut food beyond what we can do with our bare hands, to a pill to extend our mental focus.

Probably this is something we take for granted, but if you make a list all the tools that you use on a daily basis, you may be surprised by the size of the list, some are physical but many of them now live on the digital realm, some are "useful" some probably not, some have only one utility but most of them have plenty and some even have unknown usages to be discovered. The key point is that our lives will be much more difficult, to say the least, without the use of any tool.

Mastering some of these tools opens a world of new possibilities beyond what we can do with our own biological starting point.

Another key factor is related to the environments we create, develop and live in, since they also draw possibilities and limitations to what we can do, and how we can do it.

We live our lives in a mix of natural and artificial environments we build, and each of them comes with set of properties from the physical space itself, to the materials it is made of, or the characteristics of its inhabitability. Our range of actions won't be the same in the North Pole, in a desert, or for example in a megacity vs the country, and they also connect deeply to our mental status.

To sum up we can say that **our bodies, our minds, our tools, and the environments we inhabit influence our human behaviors that shape what we can do and therefore what we can automate.**

Also, our quest to create Automata's of many kinds is not new, from the earliest "computer" devices, like the 2,000 years old Antikythera mechanism, to the mechanistic devices from the middle ages or the masterworks of *Leonardo Davinci.*

To the birth of Cybernetics in 1948 by the Swedish-American pioneer polymath *Norbert Wiener*[34], author of several books that kickstarted the discipline like "Cybernetics: Or Control and Communication in the Animal and the Machine." or "The Human Use of Human Beings.", to finally the modern marvels of our time that we will explore in the following chapters.

Why we need to automate?

It is a good beginning to have a few building blocks to understand the underlying structure, the rules and procedures that govern our human bodies and minds.

But wait, why we need in the first place to have machines doing something that we can already do? why don't we outsource machines only the things we could not do?

I think nature can answer that question, **if something is "possible", nature will always find a way**. And now we are building machines with capabilities that match and even surpass our own, the "**extended new nature**" as I call it, will find its way.

I use that term since the machines we are creating are a sub product of the "original nature" or us, only breaking some of its limits. More so when they acquire, in the future, for example the ability to self-replicate without human intervention or to keep evolving without us in the loop too.

Anyway, I know it is a controversial topic, or even an oxymoron, and it goes against some of the accepted definitions of the word "nature".

Getting back to the subject, **trying to limit the capabilities of the artificial intelligence machines that we are creating is not a wise option**, maybe at the beginning of the automation journey it will be possible, but anyway a bad option, since the real impact of the limitations will be reflected in terms of reducing competitiveness, others will have machines without these auto imposed limits, reaching its true potential.

I am not suggesting that these machines, at least at the beginning, when it is still possible, shouldn't be taught to understand some of what we call ethics and moral, this is something we need to imprint as much as we can.

Since **we are in the process of teaching machines not just coding them, and this is a fundamental shift**. And the reason why it is critical that **nobody is underrepresented** on this transition, and why we all should take an active role in it.

The problem comes when people dismiss the current reality of learning machines and its abilities to surpass human capabilities, for now this is true, just in a few narrow domains, but at some point it will be in all the imaginable domains, and the worst of it, is that some people are still in denial, thinking that this is just a unprovable possibility or a long term future projection they will not live to see.

I decided that this book is needed not because is something that could happen to humanity, but because it is already happening, and many people are just not aware of it, and many other see it as simply a new trend, like others in the past.

It is happening, and it is sad to see, that many corporations sell this new revolution as a way to help and augment humans in the workforce, true in the very short term, but hiding or omitting the real impact at mid-term where it will transition to a highly probable full replacement of humans in most of the tasks, only to be delayed by regulations since the development of the enabling technologies will come at a faster pace.

We can't be prepared for something we don't know about, or that we are misled by others, due to a short term, many times interested, or naive view of the subject.

One the most common types of "blindness" is the one to gradual changes that we miss. The problem is that missing this one is not an option if we want to survive.

Yes, survive is the right word, **we are creating machines that one day will become the next us**, and the process is critical in terms of the values that will be transmitted, that's why we all must be part of it.

Maybe someday, in a not so distant future, probably in less than 15 years we will need to decide if we want to augment our biology with technology to cope up with the new artificial intelligence beings that we have created.

But until that moment, that will be, by the way, a fundamental one in human history, and again will be a gradual shift, it is important, at least, to see that it is coming, before it is too late.

Machines, at least now, are learning from us, that's why it is critical to don't leave anyone behind, so again none is underrepresented.

Machines learn from data, and if data is unbalanced, biased or inaccurate, it will lead to catastrophic consequences, that could be avoided if we were all aware and proactive in this turning point in time.

We need to have our views and perspectives included to the corpus of data that will be used to train machine learning algorithms, before it is too late, and the learning models created are very difficult to change.

Also, it is a unique opportunity to be part of the discussions that will take place to shape our future and the future of the generations to come.

It is the time to join or create think tanks to foster these conversations, and together find the best approach to tackle the challenging present and future we will live.

There are a lot of things to be done, and it should not be left alone to the technologists, scientists, a few powerful people and corporations to decide, since what we are doing today, will impact us all and define the future.

So, **we need all to automate not only to cope up with the speed of our world but to preserve and transmit our unique-ness, our essence and our accumulated wisdom, to the generations (human or not) to come**.

In the field of Artificial Intelligence one the fascinating topics is the concept of **never-ending learning systems**, something not yet achieved, at least at human level performance, and far from it in the near term, and not even fully understood at the theoretical level.

Some of my own research, through the deep learning algorithms and framework I am building, which I called "Universal Learning Machine", still in the lab works, tries to recreate some of the basic behaviors we know about human learning, since the current Artificial Intelligence systems, that we use in our daily lives, are very good at a narrow and limited activity but don't generalize so far to the full plethora of possibilities a human being is capable of.

If we take a close look to nature, the concept of evolution follows a similar path, **creatures evolve to adapt, survive and thrive in a diverse, challenging and changing environment**.

And to achieve that, **learning is one of the critical abilities to have**, in fact the creatures that evolved to learn were the ones better fitted to continue.

To some degree all species have it, at least in the reward vs punishment scenario, if they repeat their mistakes, the consequences could be too negative or even fatal to survival. If so and extrapolating it to all the members of a specie or to a branch of it, could mean the end of it, effectively cutting its branch in the evolution tree.

Since we live in a dynamic environment, the need to continuous adaptation is simply a paramount of survival, even for us humans who have tried over the last millennia to control and predict it, with some degree of success, or to be more precise "belief" of success, since the variability of our environment is, at least with our current technology, far from being fully predictable or tuned to our will.

Luckily for us we have developed environments and rules so we have the "feel" of control and so most of our time can be devoted to other more empowering activities instead of just use it for pure survival, but it doesn't mean that we have fully tamed it at all.

With this in mind, our necessity to keep learning and adapting is critical to survive as many of the possible futures we may end at.

Since one of our more precious assets is time, it is also paramount that we keep optimizing it, so we can do more with less time.

That is why for me **the main root of automation is our need to keep learning at the same speed as our world evolves too**, and this is precisely linked to our survivability in the long term, even if that means that we will end transcending to "something" we have created, something that was for us just as a tool at the beginning. At some point in time in the future, next generations will not be precisely what we understand today as "human".

From Tasks to Actions

Moving on to a more practical approach of what we can do in the short term and the essence of this new wave of automation is **delegating onto a machine most of what we do**.

Delegating what we do to machines, implies on our side a high degree of trust in "them", a similar trust is also needed when we delegate something to a fellow human, something by the way, hard to accomplish many times.

Besides trust the critical factors are selecting what we want to automate and translating it to something understandable by machines, until the communication with them will be seamless someday.

For automation to be successful we need to have a clear view of the tasks we perform and then go to a deeper level of detail to find the individual minimal actions that we use to build our complex behavior.

In this journey they key principle is **finding the right mappings of the things we do or think in our physical or mental world into the digital domain**.

For that let me first define an arbitrarily structure to narrow down the building blocks of what we do:

A **Task** is something performed or to be performed by someone or something with some utility or not, that has a start and an end, and that can be reduced to smaller subtasks in order to be finished.

A **Subtask** is a way to organize tasks in smaller units, it also has a start and an end, can be layered without limit to create levels of depth, can have interdependencies with one or several other Subtasks, and could be shared between tasks.

An **Action** is the minimum unit in which a Subtask can be divided, in our own arbitrary description, basically we could go no deeper (theoretically) in order to describe what is done to accomplish it. An action can be physical or not, and also has a start and an end.

Tasks, Subtasks and Actions can be recursive, meaning that you may need to iterate them several times.

The simple architecture is like this:

Task > Subtasks > Actions

Let's illustrate it with an example:

Task: Writing a book.

Subtasks: Topic selection, Documentation, Brainstorm ideas, Create index, Populate chapters, Find images to tell stories, Draw graphs, Find a cover, Find reviewers, Find publisher, Present book, Market book.

Actions of "Documentation Subtask": Search books by topic, Read books, Extract list of takeaways from books, same three actions with a magazine articles, videos, podcasts and patents.

As you can see there is no unique distinction of task vs subtask, or even subtask vs action , it all depends on the level of abstraction you want to use, the idea is to use a framework with enough descriptiveness so what you do can be replicated. Also think that the action level most of the times could also be subdivided, but we need to stop at some point.

Using this basic building blocks, you can generate almost infinite possibilities for the given task to map, and the flow of how it is executed can also have plenty of possibilities, a few of them could be:

1.- Sequential execution.
2.- Parallel execution.
3.- A mix of the above.
4.- Iterative executions.
5.- Repetitive but not sequential executions.

There can be many others, but most of them can be built combining these, let's explore what is the basic structure of these five examples:

1.- A Subtask and/or Actions may be executed **sequentially** in time:

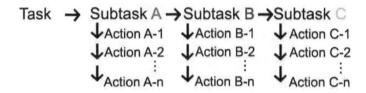

Here, there is a unique flow of execution (the arrows), and the previous action or subtask needs to be finished before the next one can start.

For simplicity, from now on will use this notation in the examples (T) for Task, (S) for Subtask and (A) for Actions.

A example of a sequential execution could be:

(T) App Design →
1.- (S) Specifications →
    1.1.- (A) Select Platform →
    1.2.- (A) Select Language →
    1.3.- (A) Define Objectives →
2.- (S) Design →
    2.1.- (A) Story board →
    2.2.- (A) Screen design →
    2.3.- (A) Icon design →
3.- (S) Coding →
    3.1.- (A) Backend side →
    3.2.- (A) Client side →
    3.3.- (A) Testing →
    3.4.- (A) Deploy →

Anyway, this example in current coding standards will not be performed linearly, but iterating over and over, using Agile or similar methodologies.

2.- Other possibility is having a **parallel** execution:

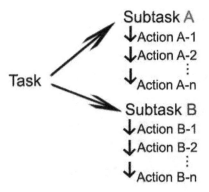

When I say parallel is usually "virtually" in parallel, because without technology (or peers) our human multitasking is usually not very feasible, anyway this could be valid also for Actions, Subtasks or even Tasks.

The inner workings a restaurant or a kitchen is a typical example of parallel Subtasks. (I use this symbol ‖ to note that they go in parallel)

(T) Restaurant Works →

‖→1.(S) Kitchen works→
    1.1.- (A) Cut Raw Food →
    1.2.- (A) Cook Food→
    1.2.- (A) Plating→
‖→2.-(S) Table works
    2.1.- (A) Setup Table →
    2.2.- (A) Get and Serve Order→
    2.3.- (A) Billing→

3.- We can also **mix** parallel and sequential execution:

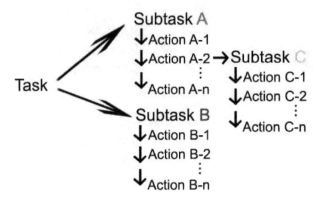

In this example "Subtask C" starts at the end of "Action A-2", again this is a theoretical case, only possible through the use of technology or with other people's help, since **our life, due to the capricious behavior of time, seems to flow sequentially**.

But the exercise of thinking how should it go, if we could split time and do several things in parallel is a good one, since once we start automating, machines can do multitasking, (usually also virtual, but very fast), and of course we can have several machines doing stuff in real parallel.

Adding to the previous example, here with several subtasks, triggered to be executed in parallel:

(T) Restaurant Works →
‖→1.(S) Kitchen works→
    1.1.- (A) Cut Raw Food →
    1.2.- (A) Cook Food ‖→
        3.1.- (S) Prepare Appetizers ‖→
        3.2.- (S) Prepare Main courses ‖→
        3.3.- (S) Prepare Deserts ‖→
    1.2.- (A) Plating→
‖→2.-(S) Table works
    2.1.- (A) Setup Table →
    2.2.- (A) Get and Serve Order→
    2.3.- (A) Billing→

4.- Other usual condition is that one or several of the subtasks or actions are needed to be performed several times (with humans sequentially and potentially with machines in parallel), in other words we **repeat or iterate** (x) times a given subtask or action

Task → Subtask A
↓Action A-1
5t ↻ Action A-2
⋮
↓ Action A-n

In this example the Action A-2 is repeated 5 times before proceeding with the next Action in this subtask.

This is one the key areas to map correctly when we find actions or subtasks that are repeated constantly in time as we will explore later in this chapter.

For example:

(T) Drug Design →
1.- (S) Drug Research →
    1.1.- (A) Preclinical testing →
    1.2.- (A) Clinical Studies ↻ 5t→
    1.3.- (A) Deployment →

Here the "Clinical Studies" Action is repeated (↻) 5 times.

5.- A variation of the previous example happens when the **repetition is not sequential** in the same subtask, but it is shared between different subtasks, or could be at another point in time in the same subtask, effectively meaning that that action is something common, and a good thig to spot when are automating.

Task   → Subtask A →Subtask B →Subtask C
          ↓Action A-1   ↓Action B-1   ↓ Action C-1
          ↓Action A-2   ↓Action A-2   ↓ Action A-2
          ↓ ⋮   ↓ ⋮   ↓ ⋮
          ↓Action A-n   ↓Action B-n   ↓ Action C-n

You can notice that "Action A-2" is repeated in Subtasks A, B and C.

Of course, this could happen even between different Tasks, so you have Subtasks and/or Actions that are repeated over and over. In fact, it is curious to discover how often this may happen.

In the next example, all the Actions are indeed repeated but at different subtask:

(T) Supermarket Stock Refill→
1.- (S) Bakery →
   1.1.- (A) Check Stock App →
   1.2.- (A) Order Products →
   1.3.- (A) Refill →
2.- (S) Seafood →
   1.1.- (A) Check Stock App →
   1.2.- (A) Order Products →
   1.3.- (A) Refill →
3.- (S) Meat →
   1.1.- (A) Check Stock App →
   1.2.- (A) Order Products →
   1.3.- (A) Refill →

To create your own map of Task, Subtasks and Actions, you can start with a big sheet of paper, good to visualize it, and a good first draft to create your mind map.

But just after that, my advice will be to use an existing software to help you with it, for example with a simple spreadsheet, where you can use one column for Tasks other for Subtasks and other for Actions, also good as a first digital draft, but not advised for big relationships between Subtasks and Actions, since it can get very messy.

Or even better a software that can manage easily the connections between your mapped items, like Microsoft Visio, Google Drawings or SmartDraw.

Microsoft Visio   Google Drawings   SmartDraw

There are also many software tools, to be found in the category of "mind mapping" in any app store that could do a decent job making your life easier translating conceptually your actions, subtasks, and tasks into digital format, life for example Simplemind.

Simplemind[35]

And will be great to have a big archive of common Tasks, like a Wikipedia where everyone can share their Tasks, Subtasks and Actions and could be easily imported by anyone to start with.

Useful, but only valid to start with, since probably your way of doing things is to some degree unique, and that is in principle a good thing, even if it is optimizable. Also, how several people do the same thing can hold many insights to learn from.

The difficult part, as in many things in life, is starting, there are 2 approaches to do it

1.- **Bottom up**, by enumerating all the tasks that you perform in a small time frame, for example a typical single day like:

Wake up & Shower
Breakfast
Review Emails
Write book
Code Algorithms
Lunch
Board Meeting
Sport
Dinner
Watch documentary
Reading
Sleep

This could cover the full picture of what to you, or you can narrow it to a specific area of your interest, like work related only, that will be explored in depth on chapter two. My take will be to start with everything you can at first, since the automation and optimization can permeate to many facets of your life, areas where you could benefit, if you automate.

Once we start describing what we do on a daily basis, we can go to bigger timeframes, to find patterns in several weekdays, months and even a year to have the whole picture.

2.- But you can do it also **top down** and start at a year or month time frame and keep narrowing down until you reach the day level, or even to a smaller timeframe, for example starting at the overview of what you do over a year:

Q1 Production works.
Q2 Research & Development works.
Q3 Production works.
Q4 Marketing works.

And then go down until you reach a smaller time frame.

Either of the 2 approaches is valid to start and depends if you're a "**synthesizer**" and feel more comfortable with the bottom up approach or you are a "**explainer**" and you prefer the top down approach.

Anyway, starting with the opposite of what you think you are, may help you find new correlations and groupings, in fact the exercise is a self-discovery one, that needs to be addressed systematically to avoid getting into mind loops. For that, **avoid if possible any judging in this phase**, since it can set your mind in a state of trying to fix whatever you find, if so write it down, so you can fix it in a later round.

Once you have your first coarse full map, you can try to **refine it adding detail** and getting into a deeper level of descriptiveness.

There is no fix good number of Tasks, Subtasks and Actions to start with, but I usually recommend the rule of a maximum of 10, meaning start with a max of 10 Tasks, max of 10 Subtasks each and max of 10 Actions each, so you end up with a maximum of 1000 "items" if they are not repeated and if you expand them all, something that usually doesn't happen, since you will probably focus in a few Tasks to start with, and don't expand them all.

It is also probable that some tasks may end becoming subtasks or even Actions, since there is no fix definition to follow, it is good that you find the one that better suits with what you do, so in fact it is a personal a unique way to describe it, that simply helps you to frame it.

Also remember that you can go to deeper levels if you need it, so for example a Subtask is composed of other Subtasks instead of Actions directly, like the example we see earlier.

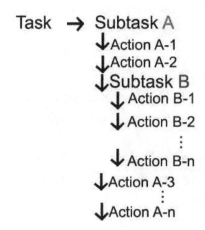

Until you have implemented a consistent methodology, a good trait is to have strong will power, in the future we could be using customized tools to help us track our behavior, meanwhile most of the workshops I have lectured about this, the majority of people found easier starting from the small timeframe, since it is easier to remember and describe in detail.

But in order to find the best tasks to automate you need to go all the way up to bigger timescales. So, you have the overview vision and discover the patterns.

To achieve a good overview, follow the next two steps once you have built your full mind map:

1.- **Enumerate** in a separate document or spreadsheet each Task and Subtasks you perform.

2.- **Count** the number of times you perform each Task & Subtasks over a day, week, month and year, and calculate the totals.

If there are few occurrences of tasks, then go to a deeper level with subtasks or even individual actions.

A simple example at the task level should look like this:

Tasks	Daily Rep	Days x Week	Weeks x Month	Months x Yr	Total
A	5	3	2	6	180
B	1	2	4	3	24
C	1	1	1	10	10
D	3	5	1	1	15

Automation is not only finding the things that we spend more time doing but also the things that we repeat over and over, with the goal of having a machine doing it for us the next time, this way we can do other things instead, and become more productive in the process.

You can create a custom list that work for handling your Tasks, but my tip is that whatever format or medium, try to use it daily or as often as you can, so you can track in real time what are you doing, and then as we will explore in the following chapters, **systematically analyze, understand and automate it.**

Looking for Repetitions

The **automation journey is all about finding what you do more than once**, in fact it is the key step.

Once you have a clear view of the set of tasks, subtasks and actions, and have figured out its repetitions, the next step is to short them in order of the impact they will have if automated.

The simpler option will be to use **just the number of repetitions** as the defining factor to short them out, and many times it will be the best approach, but take into account these two factors:

1.- The Average time used.
2.- The Automation Impact Factor (AIF).

Let's review this in detail:

1.- The **average time it takes to perform** each of the repetitions of each task, subtask or action, usually and more less, will be the same, sometimes the first repetition will take more time, and in some cases the time is variable and depends on some other related task, subtask or action, that precedes it, or that runs in parallel to it. Try to find the average time anyway, and then write it down, you can use minutes, hours or other time frames

2.- What I coined as **"The Automation Impact Factor"** or AIF for short, which is a multiplier, used to handle other things like the relationship with different tasks, subtasks or actions, the cost it take to perform it, the resources it uses, the difficulty to automate it, and why not, feel free to include other things that are important for you, maybe for your specific use case adding other factors will make sense.

Basically, AIF is a multiplier, a number from -10 to 10 being between 1 and 10 a positive degree of automatability, with 10 as the most critical to automate as soon as possible and zero or all the negative values things not to automate yet.

This way even if a task is only performed a few times a month but has a very high impact factor could come on top to be the first thing to automate.

The formula looks like this:

AIF = Relations + Cost + Resources – Difficulty.

Relations: is a number between 0 and 2, where 0 is a lonely task, subtask or action and 2 if many others depend on this one to start or feed from it, you can also use it to reflect if the results of this task, subtask or action are used by a third party.

Cost: is a number between 1 and 5, where 1 would be almost no relative cost to perform it and 5 if this is the main cost in all of your budget, budget by the way can be a mix of money and time, this is a relative value you feel comfortable with.

Resources: is a number between 0 and 3, where 0 means that it doesn't consume, besides time and possibly money reflected in the Cost variable, any other physical or logical assets in order to be performed, and 3 if it is relatively a high consumer of your available resources. The idea here is to relate this value to all the other task, subtasks or actions, so the numbers are proportional, you also need to find your own balance for it.

Difficulty (to be automated, not of the task, subtask or action itself): is a number between 0 and 10, where 0 would be very easy to automate, and 10 almost impossible, maybe due to the lack of existing technology to automate it, or due to regulations that forbid it, or because it will incur in a huge cost to be automated. If the task, subtask or action is physical I usually start this factor with 1 or more instead of 0. My goal is that once you finish this book you will have a better sense to start measuring this value.

Bear in mind that **some of these factors may vary over time**, depending for example on market conditions, availability of technology or resources, regulations and other aspects. So, it is good advice to revisit periodically your "automation documents" and also keep yourself updated about the status of this developing field.

AIF = Relations + Cost + Resources − Difficulty.

The result of the AIF could be less than 1, meaning that the task, subtask or action will be quite hard to automate.

Once you have the AIF or Automation Impact Factor, you can use my **Automatability Score** Formula to include the time and repetitions:

Automatability Score = Number of **repetitions** x average **time** per repetition x **Automation Impact Factor (AIF)**.

The time frame used is important and depends on the scope, for example if you are tracking the automatability at the Task level and all the Tasks are repeated at least once a month, then "number of repetitions per month" will be a good choice, but depending on your case, could be per year too. If you are at the Subtask or Action level maybe "repetitions per day" will be better.

The key point is to **use the time frame, that matches your least repeated**, otherwise you will need to use fractions to have consistent values, across all the repetitions you are measuring.

Regarding the average time per repetition, again for the unit of measure, a wise choice is to use the smallest one that is meaningful, usually minutes, but can be seconds, or hours, or even days at the Task level, but it is not usual, unless your level of abstraction is very high.

Selecting your level of detail is good to **avoid mixing Tasks with Subtasks and Actions**, have different documents for each of them, since the time frames could change, if you want to make a better sense of the data you are dealing with, my advice will be, when possible, treat them always separately so at all the scales, the numbers are consistent. You can have as much documents to track this as needed.

Also, a good advice is to start from the Action level, since it is the deepest level and probably easier to start automating.

Let's explore it with the following example, so you can see the implications of the different variables:

Let's start with the Automation Impact Factor (AIF):

Action	Relations (0-2)	Cost (1-5)	Resources (0-3)	Difficulty (0-10)	Automation Impact Factor (AIF)
A-1	0	1	0	0	1
A-2	2	3	1	3	3
A-3	1	1	0	0	2
A-4	1	1	0	9	-7

In the "A-2" action the calculations will be:

Automation Impact Factor (AIF) for the action named "A-2" = 2 (Relations) + 3 (Cost) + 1 (Resources) − 3 (Difficulty) = 3.

And so on with the other actions.

Now let's calculate the **Automatability Score**:

Action	Repetitions	Average Time	Automation Impact Factor (AIF)	Automatability Score
A-1	10	5	1	50
A-2	3	100	3	900
A-3	100	2	2	400
A-4	100	2	-7	-1400

Remember that the **Automatability Score** of the action and the Automation Impact Factor (AIF) columns are calculated with the formulas described earlier.

You can see that the first action that will be best to automate here is "A-2" since it has the highest Automatability Score, even being the least repeated one, only 3 times, but since The Automation Impact

Factor (AIF) is high and the average time needed to perform each repetition is high, it leads to a very high Score.

So, the **Automatability Score** for action "A-2" is = 3 (Repetitions) * 100 (Average Time) * 3 (AIF) = 900.

Action	Number of Repetitions	Average Time	Relations (0-2)	Cost (1-5)	Resources (0-3)	Difficulty (0-9)	AIF	Automat ability Score
A-1	10	5	0	1	0	0	1	50
A-2	3	100	2	3	1	3	3	900
A-3	100	2	1	1	0	0	2	400
A-4	100	2	1	1	0	9	-7	-1400

On the other end of the score index, we have the "A-4" Action, with the same time and repetitions as "A-3" but looks like it is very hard task to automate, with a Difficulty of 9, moving its Automation Impact Factor (AIF) to the lowest factor of -7:

Automation Impact Factor (AIF) for the action named "A-4" = 1 (Relations) + 1 (Cost) + 0 (Resources) − 9 (Difficulty) = -7.

And so, its final Automatability score is -1400, being the worst one, and probably a very bad choice to start automating.

Here is the math for the **Automatability Score** for action "A-4" = 2 (Repetitions) * 100 (Average Time) * -7 (AIF) = -1400.

As you can see the math is simple, what is more complex is finding the right values, but as many things in life, experience is the key to master it.

Anyway remember to revisit the tables periodically, since some of the factors could change over time, and something that is hard to automate now, could be easier in the future, through the book we will explore other tips on how to estimate this, and again **experience** as always, **is the best teacher** here.

When looking for repetitions, the preferred way is to record them in a digital format, so the calculations are "automated" too, numbers and the math used here is very simple, but easier is if it is already done, you can find a zip file with the example spreadsheets in my web site http://www.vivancos.com/automate/samples.zip

To sum up, **repetitions are at the core of any automation process, train yourself to spot them**, but have in mind that you play against your own brain, since it likes repeating stuff that had worked in the past, and also remember that are many other factors influencing the automatability of any task, subtask or action, like the time used for each repetition or the described Automation Impact Factor.

Becoming a Dataset

Once we have a clear picture of what is worth automating and what should be automated first in order to achieve the most impactful results, the next big question is: how to start the automation process? , do I need to be a data scientist or a roboticist to do it?

Well if you are, it is a great capability to have nowadays, and for some scenarios you will need us to help you with the process, but increasingly there are many situations where automation is possible without the intervention of experts in the field.

In fact, from the main building blocks of automation, you probably already have one of them, built in:

Automation = Data + Algorithms + Computing.

For physical tasks a fourth ingredient is needed:

Automation = Data + Algorithms + Computing + **Robotics.**

Did you find what you may already have?

With a simple look at the formulas, looks like there is no human in the loop, but usually the opposite is true, in fact since this book is mostly about automating human tasks, we need humans to learn from, and that's where the "data" part comes to play.

The true power of Artificial Intelligence relies on understanding the world at a deeper level than us, but for that we need to provide it **with data to learn from**.

Oversimplifying the process, you gather data, when you have enough, you group it into a **training data set** so machine learning algorithms can **learn** from it and build a **"model" of you data**, so next time you have new data the model is used to interpret it.

That's why it is key to convert what is physical in the world to the digital realm of data or bytes, this is the essence of the digitization process so trendy nowadays.

But beyond trends it is something we need to start to embrace, the sooner we start and the wider the data we were able to capture from ourselves and from our interactions the better off we will end.

In fact this has been the critical factor for all the startups that have changed the world in the last few decades, they gather, understand and make use of (mostly our) data, and so they build an economic empire and transform traditional sectors.

In 2006 mathematician *Clive Humby*[36] said, or at least the phrase was credited to him, that "**Data is the new oil**", and now we can clearly see that the economic value and impact in our society of "data" is even bigger to what oil did, and still does.

But my proposal goes beyond the organizations that already are making money out of it, I think that we need all to capture as much data as we can and as soon as possible.

You need to **take control of your data**, from all your past interactions in the digital world, to all your current activities, **be your own producer of data and become a "dataset".**

When I say "you", is because it should start at the personal level, but it is also true for corporations or public organizations.

When you think about the "data" you produce on a personal basis, maybe what comes to mind, are pictures & videos and a few documents, but it should go way beyond that.

There are two main data sources:

1.- Data that is still in the analog or **physical world** without any interaction with the digital domain.

2.- Data that is **already** flowing through **digital** means.

For the first scenario, it is true that even today, most of what happens in the physical world is not digitized, and therefore it is not "usable" data, but it holds an unmeasurable amount of insights and value once it is digitized and analyzed.

For example, our hear rate, or many other vital measures like our brain waves, our physical activity, our sugar levels, blood pressure or even our changing microbiome[37], to name a few, if studied in advance can help us improve our health or even prevent a fatal event. But we usually don't have sensors capturing this data on a regular basis, and therefore this data is basically lost.

Or our own voice, is usually not recorded 24/7, at least that we are aware of, and also may hold a lot of clues from health related, discovering behavioral patterns or for memory augmentation to name a few.

And if you go beyond, for example our facial expressions or a full 360 video of our actions in the world, could also explain many things, even if it is seen as a dystopian scene from a science fiction artwork, we have now more cameras than ever before recording with or without our knowledge, not only from governments and institutions but from billions of smartphones too.

There are several possible issues regarding getting all what happens in the physical world into digital bytes, the first one is security, also the availability/readiness of the technology to capture it, but also and very important too that it is **seamlessly integrated with us**.

Nowadays it is true that we have many commercial sensors and devices to measure almost anything, but they are usually too bulky, compromising or even altering our behaviors while "wearing" them, or they are too expensive, or the resolution they have is very poor.

So, there are still challenges to overcome in this regard.

Our capacity to store data has increased exponentially while the cost has shirked, being almost free for some "small" scales, but still expensive for high volumes or "Big Data", something that by the way is also linked mostly to technology development. the data storage that we could buy 10 years ago for say 100$ we can buy it today for 10$ or less.

If fact it is a never ending race, since as we increase the resolution of our sensors and devices, we also increase the size needed to store and transmit them, so we need higher capacity storage devices and also increase the speed of our networks to cope up.

In 1990 when I was developing graphics software for games and apps, I worked with very low resolution displays & images of about 320 x 200 pixels or less (0.06 Megapixels), low resolution in today's terms, at that time was incredible to see that details and in a few colors since we just have left the monochrome world in computing.

Now 30 years later I work with "8K" displays with 7680x4320 pixels (or 33 Megapixels) and take pictures with a Smartphone with a 108 Megapixel sensor or (12032 x 9024 pixels) , an even so we are far away from the visual acuity of our own eyes, estimated to have about 500 Megapixels of resolution.

So regardless of the never ending race for improving the resolution of our captures, **if we could store data from all our modalities, activities, and "sensors"**, it will mean that we will have a better picture, not only of our health but also of our behavior, and in fact **will be the key to improve it**.

Some examples could be: what we see, what we ear, what we speak, what we smell, what we taste, what we feel with our skin like temperature or pressure, our muscle movements, our heart rate, our brain waves, and many others.

On the mental side, our mental activities, our emotions, what we recall, what we predict and so on.

This does not mean that we should be wearing sensors at every moment or manually feeding data to what I call **our "data layer"**, in fact it should be seamless to avoid altering it, and instead of reaching the goal of optimizing our time, we end wasting it. So, finding the right tradeoff is critical, but also revising it every now and then, since new technology could help us achieve something previously thought to be impossible.

On the **second scenario, where data already flows in the digital world**, in theory should be easier to keep track of our digital life, own it and store it in our terms.

But the problem is that for most of the data is not so easy, since it is at the core of the business models of the startups that rule the digital world, and won't be so eager to share it all, even if it is the data that you have created with their "free" or paid app.

It means that since it is true that we leave plenty of digital trails of our activities on the net, or "digital tattoos" in words of *Juan Enriquez*[38], the difficulty comes on how to access them and download them at your will.

Juan Enriquez TED Talk[39]

Also, there are many other interaction points with technology, that probably are not even stored, since they are performed while not connected, and also because there are no rewards for those app developers to enable its recording and storage.

The best scenario, in terms of digital storage of our actions, all the activities that we perform in our digital devices like computers, smartphones, smartwatches, smart TVs and alike should be stored as **a timeline of what we do**.

A timeline because we could see all these actions as events in time, that once feed to the right algorithm could draw insights regarding to our behavior and can lead to optimization and automation of our digital interactions.

Connecting with the previous physical scenario, of course we can add existing sensor data to that physical "life" timeline and extend that way, the gathered information about any "event".

It is also true that again security and privacy should be on top of it, and it is something that will take time for some typologies of data, but if dealt correctly could lead to huge advantages. Something similar happened at the early days of the Internet, took some time for all of us to change our mindset and trust, from buying goods online to doing on-line banking.

There are a few companies that are already working on tracking and replicating some of our actions in the digital domain, mostly related to automation of repetitive tasks, but why not, with a possible link with to the subject matter of this book.

They are the so called RPA (Robotic Process Automation) tools, with the "robot" word you may think that they are mostly for physical tasks, but it is the opposite, they are mostly used in the software world, we will explore some of them in the next chapter about automating your work.

Becoming a dataset is one the key takeaways from this book, because **machines learn from data**, if there is no data they can't build models, so **unless your data is there to reflect what, how and who you are, you will be left apart** in the models created by machines to understand the world.

It is not only a matter of automation only, the implications of not capturing your data span beyond it, since time flows in one direction only, so data not captured will mean data lost, and so insights and valuable information with it.

CHAPTER TWO:

Automate My Work

Do we need to work?

The amount of time we humans usually "work", has varied from the early humans "hunters" to our current "hyperconnected" world (at least digitally, since the Covid-19 outbreak, the physical connection sadly is not as flamboyant as it was), from maybe a debatable couple hours a day for stone age early humans hunters to take care of the "basics", to 16+ hour workday for some current jobs, maybe because they need it to survive and some others with the "workaholic" label.

We work for several reasons, but the main universal one is **to earn a living**, or to **satisfy our most basic needs** like shelter, food intake, healthcare and for a few, ideally should be for all, as one of the key ingredients **to give meaning to life itself**.

Through history a life without the need to work, per se, has been the pursue of many and the privilege earned or inherited of a few.

And something achieved, by some people, also at the end of life, only in the last couple centuries, and only in some countries, thanks to public retirement plans or private ones.

Sometimes these retirements came at a time when the health of the individuals is compromised and thus the lack of work can't be fully enjoyed.

If we have the possibility of designing and implementing new models for our societies from the ground up, won't make much sense to include the need to work per se, at least if the end product of "working", in terms of covering the basics, can be achieved through other means.

In these new models of societies, we may need to figure out a way to give meaning to people's life through other activities, since the lack of something to do, could be very problematic and create other deeper problems too.

It is true that some people, where I feel included, enjoy his or her current job, and don't want or see the need to get rid of it. In fact, we don't tend to see it as "work" but something else, at least most of it.

But if we unbind the work from the economic reward derived from it, then we may be able to keep the activity to some degree and remove the need of the monetary burden, since the reward will be for example the advancement in the task performed.

And even so, I think that **you can add a new layer of meaning to what you do if you automate** as much as you can, since basically you will be able to do more of it in less time, and feel more productive per unit of your valuable time used.

We can argue that this will hold true, until time itself is commoditized thanks to advances maybe in life extension research and regenerative medicine. Something, so far, in the realm of science fiction, but probably enabled by technology in a not so distant future.

And even if we had close to infinite time, improving the efficiency of what we do in terms of resources, including time, it is a trend that has never stopped through history, even every time we have extended our lifespan.

So **"work" in the future, could be something not essential to survive, but profound changes in the fabric of our societies are needed to make this a reality**, since the current and very ingrained economic models that rule it, dictate that humans need to work to earn "money", to buy goods, to sustain corporations, to pay taxes and basically to keep the gears of our society moving. Some of this maybe questioned in the aftermath of the global Covid-19 pandemic.

So, if we find alternative ways to build our societies, we may not need to work at some point in time, but until that moment the wise choice is to automate it, so we can stay relevant and improve our efficiencies.

And meanwhile start moving towards a model of society where we all can enjoy doing **something that is meaningful**, help us **expand our innate capacities**, **enable the discovery** new ones and **contribute to a common good**.

While it may seem utopian, and it is, since work is not isolated from the rest of the facets of a society, as many things in life, it is better to start moving in the direction of your goals, than waiting for all you goals to come magically at once. The closer you get to what you want the more chances you have, to be in the realm of possible scenarios where you really achieve it at the end.

To sum up, yes **we need to work, at least for now, and the best we can do is automate it, to improve our chances of keeping it, while it last**, and have the extra time needed to **be constantly getting ready for what comes next**, instead of repeating tasks we can outsource to a machine.

What is the value of my work?

Besides the values referenced in the previous chapter, the amount of money we earn from it, should be the natural answer to the question, but it goes beyond that.

Not all the tasks that we do, have the same impact on either the productivity of what we do, or to the final outcome, in terms of completeness of the task or its impact in monetary revenue.

That is why it is critical to find out and rank each task that we perform, to try to automate first, the ones that will leverage the best outcomes or results.

And if we do this periodically, we will be improving constantly, always optimizing what we do, and trying to maximize our productivity and thus our competitiveness.

The other option or the business as usual approach may have a very short lifespan, since the alternative is that either someone else in your organization or a competing company will do it, and probably taking you out of business in the process.

So, **for companies to survive the quest for automation is a survival need**, way beyond a current fancy trend.

And for the employee too, since the inherent value of any work is closely related, in the end, to the impact it has in the profits of the organization as a whole.

Some people may think that their job, does not impact the results of the company where he or she works, but if the management and the underlaying organization layers involved bellow it, have done its job, no worker will be just decoration in any organization.

Of course, all the organizations don't do this the right way, but in the private sector they won't last long and sadly with them the poorly managed people working there.

So, if you find yourself in one of them maybe a good advice to start looking for alternatives, before it is too late.

This holds true, by the way, from small to big corporations, only the later may last longer due to existing economic resources, patents or other means, and sadly we have plenty of examples of the survival rate of organizations in the past, *Simon Sinek*[40] explore some of the reasons brilliantly in his book "The Infinite Game".

In another realm are the public companies managed by government entities, there some may wrongly believe they have no competitors, so it could be easier to find inefficiencies and legacy jobs still being performed.

I think the even these entities must compete, maybe for the budgets or due to the election terms that usually come with changes in the management or with the right approach they should do it with other countries or with other regions.

Ideally it will be more cooperation than competition or maybe coopetition, but until that moment becomes a reality, public institutions usually need to compete for resources at least.

So also, if you work for a public entity is a very good approach to automate as much as you can, so you can help the end the goal of making your country better.

And if you find out, that what you do is becoming obsolete, also will be good to try to do as much as you can to change it. You may think that you have your salary granted, in theory for life, and you could be right, but maybe not, and besides that, giving meaning to what you do is always a good strategy.

Also if you work at an NGO, what you do, probably has already a profound meaning for you, so there you have a great "value" already, so optimizing your time, you can reach and help more people, or doing it better is just a great objective to pursue.

Being in a public or private institution, as long as you get paid, you can use the salary you get from your job is a first indicator of the inherent "value" it has, at least for your employer, many employees think they are underpaid, and on the other side many companies use minimum possible wages to optimize profits, so it is easy to find salaries that don't reflect the real value generated by the work being performed, but anyway is a baseline you can use to measure it, even if it is no perfect or even fair.

Another good question to ask is, **what would happen if this job is not done?** Or in other words what is the relationship between the work you perform and the value it generates for rest of the organization.

If the answer is nothing, it is interesting to ask again and think it through, since that answer usually comes due to oversimplification, if you look deeper, you may spot, not so apparent connections between your job and other aspects or areas of the organization. If you are sure it is still nothing, again is a good advice to look for alternative jobs as soon as possible.

Sometimes the job you perform is not directly linked to the economic performance of the organization, could be linked to compliance, regulations, or just be part a bigger set of tasks, anyway only inefficient organizations keep roles where there is no impact at all if a job someone is doing, is simply not done at all, remember that the impact doesn't need to be monetary.

It doesn't mean that most the of the jobs couldn't be replaced or improved, and so the older way of doing it will become obsolete, and this is probably what will happen if you keep business as usual.

So, if you want to have a mathematical formula to get the value of your job, could be the sum of what you get paid for performing it, and if you work in a private company + a fraction of the revenues (if positive) of the organization. Will be great to have a universal formula to calculate this fraction, and with the financial books of the company it could be done, otherwise your salary, or the average salary of your peers in your organization, or in similar roles in your sector could be a number to start.

In NGOs or in settings where there is no monetary reward for your job, the impact of your activities, the number of people impacted by your actions, or its results in any other terms, can be used also as a measure of "value".

But beyond your salary, the next big question is **what can you do to increase the value of your job?** and hopefully your salary too. And the answer is **going beyond what you currently do** and getting time to do so by **automating what you already do**.

Looking for Repetitions

Finding Repetitions in your activities is the key principle of the automation journey.

Usually our human approach once we he have a new task, is first to learn the basics, with time we tend to master it, then some even optimize it to do it faster, and then, optimized or not, we all keep repeating it over and over, maybe to its maximum performance, and probably to the limit of our capacities.

Good but wrong, **once you master something the next thing you need to do is finding the way to automate it so the process itself is performed by a machine instead of a human**.

But wait, they always said in my company that machines are here to help us do better our jobs, not to replace us, we will always have the final word and be the supervisors of machines. Sorry to bring the inconvenient truth, but that was the paradigm before the 2020s.

Now is **automate or be automated**, remember the mantra of the book. Now there is no room to just mastering something, now we need to become masters of automating what we do.

In a work environment we usually need to go a step beyond and automate the work of teams, if you work "solo" the previous chapter cover most of the tricks but it is usually hard to find real "solo" roles in almost any organization. And it is usually a mix of team and "solo" work.

When you need, or have, to work with other team members from your organization **the key step is defining the tasks, subtasks and actions together** and mix the ones performed individually with the ones shared with others, yes it is interesting to mix all the individual and shared, so as a team you can see the whole picture.

Usually if you dig deep enough, the "action" level should be outlined to be performed at the individual level and on the other hand most of the subtasks will be shared between team members, and of course the task most likely will be shared too.

Even if you shift turns with someone in the real world or if you work side by side in environments like the XP Extreme Programming methodology in the virtual world. There is always a way to frame the actions per person.

Repetitions could come at any of the levels, from tasks to actions, and it is fundamental to explore all the levels to find the right automation order.

Also remember that you could have many levels of subtasks and that some of them maybe shared between tasks or be repeated at a different level.

That is why it is fundamental to create the right mapping of tasks, so it is descriptive and at the end useful to draw the relationships between them and the people involved.

Really interesting insights comes when this is done with all the team members, since you can find actions that are performed by more than one person, so when you count the repetitions this is something to track too. Having someone dynamizing the process is also helpful and for big organizations the "**automation facilitator**" is a role to be created as soon as possible.

To get the most out of this, and in my experience leading automation workshops, it is best if you divide the process in the following steps:

1.- **Generate at the individual level**, without any interaction with other teammates, the **full list of Tasks, Subtasks and Actions**, it is critical to isolate this first for each individual, to avoid polluting it, it will be enriched later but you can miss valuable information in the automation process if you skip this step or mix teammates too soon.

2.- Without sharing yet the individual lists, with all the teammates **generate a global, unique and agreed list of Tasks, Subtasks and Actions**. If you are using any project management tools in your organization you can use them here to help you finding what to add, but don't use them in the previous step.

3.- **Merge the individual lists with the global list**, keeping the duplicates if any, but keeping track of them.

4.- Using the previous lists (1x Team member + 1 Global) **Build** the Following documents **for each Task**:

4.1.- "List of Team Members":

For example:

Team member 1: Rose White.

Team member 2: John Smith.

Team member 3: Mathieu Wang.

Team member 4: Abigail Murphy.

You can add their roles and skills if you want, may add value for future works, but it is not necessary at this point.

4.2.- "List of Subtasks", create a merged list, looking at each shared task:

For example:

Subtask A: Create SharePoint.

Subtask B: Update User Lists.

Subtask C: Request Authorization Rights.

Subtask D: Upload documents.

Subtask E: Fill Compliance Forms.

Depending on the "size" of the Task it is possible to have several levels of Subtasks, as exposed in chapter one, and depending on the level of abstraction or concreteness used, you could end up upgrading subtasks to tasks for example or downgrading subtasks to actions. But there is no problem at all in having layers or levels of Subtasks, my advice is to build it in several iterations until you create a document that is descriptive enough.

4.3.- "List of Team members per Subtask", build it identifying which team members participate in each Subtask:

For example:

Subtask A: Team members 1,2,3

Subtask B: Team members 2,3

Subtask C: Team members 1,4

Subtask D: Team members 1,2,3

Subtask E: Team members 1,2,3,4

This is the simplified and recommended version, since expanding it will get maybe easier to read but more difficult to see the relationships, for example with the Subtask C, it will be: "Request Authorization Rights" is done by "Rose White" & "Mathieu Wang", and so on.

You may also have Subtasks with only one team member.

4.4.- **"List of Team members per Action",** one for each Subtask, create them, doing the same as in the previous list but with the actions of each Subtask:

For example:

Actions of Subtask A "Create SharePoint":
   Action "Sales SharePoint": Team members 1,2,3
   Action "Marketing SharePoint": Team member 1
   Action "Finance SharePoint": Team members 2,3

And the same for all the Subtasks.

Since you are merging the individual list with the commonly agreed one, it is very common to find many "solo" actions and also actions that are the same in essence but different team members give them different names, if so try to **agree a unified name** here, between all the team members involved.

For example, the task unified as "Upload Documents", maybe named by a team member "Copy documents to cloud" and by other team member "Upload files to server".

For a quick review of the automation documents, and if there are not many sub-levels, I recommend using a capital letter to identify Subtasks, and numbers to identify Actions.

4.5.- **"List of Subtasks repetitions"**, like what we did in the chapter one with tasks, but at the subtask level, and adding a column for the number of team members involved in each subtask

You also need to **agree on a timeframe** to measure the repetitions, could be the total time of the task at hand or bigger timeframe, but usually not bigger than a year.

SubTasks	Number of Team Members	Daily Repetitions	Days x Week	Weeks x Month	Months x Year	Total
A	3	5	3	2	6	180
B	2	1	2	4	3	24
C	2	1	1	1	10	10
D	3	3	5	1	1	15
E	4	1	1	1	12	12

The Total is just the multiplication of Daily repetitions x Days x Weeks s Months.

And the Number of Team Members will be used later to determine the Automatability, a "Solo" Subtask or Action is usually easier to automate, but on the contrary the impact in cost and time savings when multiple team members are involved is usually greater.

Have in mind that at this point we haven't yet gone to review in detail the time used, if you think with the classical view of project management, at the subtasks level is something to track, with automation in mind is usually better to add it at the action level instead.

4.6.- **"List of Action repetitions"**, The same as the previous list but with the "Action" scope, create one for each Subtask.

4.7.- "List of Automatable Actions", as the final step, and the critical thing to do when looking for repetitions, is to frame it with the automatability lenses so we can start to automate as soon as possible.

As we also described in chapter one, the Automatability Score formula and the Automation Impact Factor (AIF) are still a great framework to decide what to automate.

When you work with teams, there are two approaches, you can **calculate it by team member**, only with the Actions they perform, and **then mix them all together** averaging the values o you can have a consensus between all the team members and **build from the beginning a single list**.

Usually when the actions are homogenized correctly this will be very easy to generate, but when each team member, fights his or her own battle, it can be very unbalanced, an action can take 1h for one member of the team, and maybe 10m to others, and this exercise could bring this unwanted reality to the table, a great moment to help improve the inefficiencies within an organization, and **avoid** one the pitfalls of having the so popular, and so harmful, **silos and keepers of the silos in corporations**.

Anyway this should not stop you to begin the automation journey, just remember that this is an iterative process, so once you have optimized the possible disparities in how each team member deals with the actions, you can re-visit the list and update what is needed.

If you use the one list per team member approach, be careful with the time units, so all use the same, this is the only thing they need to agree first, and once you have the final list merged, check if the repetitions are the same between teammates, if so just average the times, if there are big disparities in the time, it is better to take this into account, let's see this with an example:

For Action A1 "Create Sales SharePoint", we need to calculate how many repetitions each team member does and how long it takes each repetition on average:

Action A1, Team member 1:   6 repetitions, 5 minutes
Action A1, Team member 2:   2 repetitions, 5 minutes

Aggregated should be

Action A1:   **8 repetitions, of 5 minutes each**

But imagine the time it takes for each repetition is different for each team member:

Action A1, Team member 1:   6 repetitions, 10 minutes
Action A1, Team member 2:   2 repetitions, 20 minutes

Aggregated should be

Action A1:   **8 repetitions, 12,5 minutes each**

And not 15 minutes each if you just do the average between 10 and 20 minutes.

The 12,5 minutes comes from the next formula
$(6*10+2*20) / 8 = 12,5$

(6 repetitions by 10 minutes each + 2 repetitions by 20 minutes each) divided by 8 repetitions total.

So, for an action performed by only 2 team members the formula would look like this:

Time= (Rep1 * Time1 + Rep2 * Time2) / (Rep1+ Rep2)

Being:
Rep = Repetitions for team member.
Time= Time for team member.

So sometimes **just averaging could make you reach wrong conclusions**, and influence the automatability score of an action, unless the time used by each member is the same.

Regarding the Automation Impact Factor (AIF), that remember is calculated looking at the Relations, Cost, Resources & Difficulty of each action. Will be probably shared across teammates for each action but be careful because Cost & Resources may be different, and you should compensate for them.

Also, my advice regarding the "**Resources**" factor, is to reflect a higher number if the action is performed by many team members and also increase "**Cost**", this is the reason to add the number of team members involved in each action it previous documents.

This **"list of Automatable Actions"**, has the same structure as the one described in chapter one, just have in mind the considerations reflected above.

Action	Number of Repetitions	Average Time	Relations (0-2)	Cost (1-5)	Resources (0-3)	Difficulty (0-9)	AIF	Automat ability Score
A-1	10	5	0	1	0	0	1	50
A-2	3	100	2	3	1	3	3	900
A-3	100	2	1	1	0	0	2	400
A-4	100	2	1	1	0	9	-7	-1400

This is usually performed at the "Action" level and one per Subtask is needed but depending on the abstraction for some automation initiatives could be done at the "Subtask" level.

Summing up, to start the process you need:

1.- Full lists of Tasks, Subtasks and Actions at the individual level, 1 per Teammate.

2.- A Global, unique and agreed list of Tasks, Subtasks and Actions.

And with these lists, crate the following working documents **for each Task**:

1.- List of Team Members.
2.- List of Subtasks.
3.- List of Team members per Subtask.
4.- List of Team members per Action (1x Subtask).
5.- List of Subtasks Repetitions.
6.- List of Action Repetitions. (1 x Subtask)
7.- List of Automatable Actions. (1 x Subtask)

Depending on the size of your organization, or the size of the team, it is interesting to define roles in your team for the automation journey like:

Automation Worker: Responsible for developing the automation at hand, depending on the action or subtask could be someone from a technical area of the organization or not and can be outsourced to a third party.

Automation Owner: Will handle specific automation initiatives for one or several actions and/or subtasks, it is usually the beneficiary of the automation, and will report progress to the Automation Facilitator periodically, depending on the typology of the action or subtask the owner could be an Automation Worker too.

Automation Facilitator: To track progress of one or more initiatives, will stay updated on the tools for automation (explored on next subchapter), and report the status of each automation initiative to the stakeholders. Could be internal or external and could be one or more depending on the size of the organization.

Chief Automation Officer: In medium or big corporations, will oversee all the automation initiatives within the organization and report to the board & CEO, will manage the budgets needed to perform the automation of the company, depending also on the size of the company, this role can be merged with the Chief Artificial Intelligence Officer.

As you can see the journey to find repetitions in a work setting should span to all the layers of an organization, ideally to maximize its results with the direct implication of the top management to avoid ending developing again "silo" like activities that will only improve a fraction of what is really possible.

Embrace the quest to find the repetitions in your day to day work, and your chances to survive and thrive in the coming age of automation will be maximized, and better do it as a team to multiply your chances and help your business stay on top of the game.

Tools for Automation

There are several innovative startups and big corporations that have understood the value of automation and are starting to provide tools and services to cope with some of the activities that we perform when we automate.

We will divide the tools into 2 branches, that are sometimes interlinked:

Physical Tools

For the physical automation, looking for advances in robotics should be the "natural" way to go.

Robotics is not per se a new science, several industries have a long history with it, but even so, at least, at the time this book was written, it is fair to say that we are at a very early stage of its development.

Starting with how we move or how a robot should move like us, to help us automate, it is true that we have robots, like the ones from Boston Dynamics, or from Agility Robotics and a few others, that can walk more less like us and have our human scale, but so far they are not commercially available to purchase at the price of a household appliance.

Boston Dynamics[41]   Agility Robotics[42]

And besides cost, the autonomy, complexity, limited capabilities or weight are some other factors still to be resolved or improved too.

Legs to walk is not the only way to move around the world, in fact many commercially available robots, are using a plethora of other means, like wheels in the ground or rotors to flight.

Some of these robots are now extending many of our innate capacities, but still it is critical to have robots that can mimic our full range of capacities, if we want to automate all our physical actions too, and to reach that point, there are many milestones to achieve first.

For example, also our **hands and arms** are very valuable "devices" we have, that shape many of our interactions with the world and is entities.

Robotic hands and arms are also at a very early stage of development in the field, at least again at a price range small enough to make it feasible for all.

The state of the art could be the last version from the Robonaut from NASA or the humanoid robot Fedor, now renamed Skybot F-850 from the Russian Foundation for Advanced Research Projects (RFARP) .

The first a robotic "astronaut" and "cosmonaut" the later, companions at the International Space Station.

NASA's Robonaut[43]   Russia's Fedor Robot[44]

But new approaches like the ones from Shadow Robot Company, with HaptX[45] **haptic globes** to control the hands and with SynTouch[46] **tactile and biomimetic sensors.** A great contender to watch in this space.

Shadow Robot Company[47]

A race to build robots with all our physical capabilities is ongoing, so stay tuned to advances in this fascinating field if you want to cope up.

So, with this short review of the state of the art of robotics, means that we won't be able yet to automate physical tasks?

Yes we can, but only to some degree until advances in robotics match all the things we humans can do, anyway the exercise of finding out the tasks, subtasks and actions will be still be valid, but the possibility to automate it will be limited by technology.

Depending on the economic resources you have to automate, it could be feasible to get closer to the edge of what it possible or not, but it is true that **once you use research grade technology, the deployment times of automation gets harder to predict**.

But if the reward of automation is estimated to be beyond the investment needed to achieve it, maybe worth evaluating and exploring the risks in both directions.

One of the key aspects to think through here, is the initial time estimates, and the procedures to measure success.

I usually do not advice companies to get into automating physical tasks where the first measurable results are foreseen to be beyond the year timeframe.

For a simple reason it is very hard to predict with the current growth rate of technology if a given technique will be obsolete next year.

And if this is the case, the implications are devastating since there is high probability that the investment will be a waste of time and resources, with many learnings but not justifiable in terms of return of investment.

If your company has the resources to be the game changer then will be a good strategy to be the one moving the technology to the next step, and even so be ready for unknown unknowns that come when you are at the edge of what is possible. It is true that learnings could pay off, being first is rewarding but maybe not in economic terms.

From my own experience, some of the startups I have created, ended in economic failures (learnings), and one of the reasons was getting too soon: like a virtual reality company in 1995 when costs were huge and capacities of the technology quite limited, or an apps company in 2000, when smartphones were still in the realm of high end PDAs, low internet mobile connectivity and convincing consumers to do what they do today with a smartphone was like predicating in the desert, or a Nanotechnology for Space Exploration company in 2005, where nanotech developments were, and still are very slow, and the private space sector was still in its very early days.

So, beware when you move at the edge of what is possible, since you could end learning a lot, expending a lot too, but not earning a cent. If you are still brave to go there, calculate to the best of your possibilities the economics of it and find the right partners, it is true too that **big rewards** most of the times **comes with great risks taken**.

Anyway, this is not always the case, there are many other scenarios where technology already exist, the right approach is usually to buy or license it, and then customize it as needed, instead of re-inventing the wheel.

Physical automation is not only robotics per se, a lot is handled only through connected sensors.

Most of the physical tasks, subtasks or actions you may think of, can we performed with the right sensors and actuators, if they already have been invented.

Sensors are used to measure different modalities of information or "change", like visual information with visible light cameras, or sound with microphones, but there are also many other sensors like accelerometers, magnetometers, motion sensors, several gases related sensors, infrared, ultraviolet, lidars, radars, pressure, flow and many others.

An **actuator** is something that enables a physical interaction, like motors, pumps, levers, gears or valves, can be hydraulic, electric or pneumatic, comparing it with our own human body, muscles are a good example of the "device" that enables our body parts to move.

Of course, there are many other physical pieces or "Inter-Hardware", that conform the needed shape we want to mimic in our automation journey, for example in a robot the skeleton, joints and many other moving or not parts.

The art of replicating nature with technology is called **biomimetics**[48], and you could, in theory, mimic every living creature with the right resources, not only humans.

This is nothing new, in fact through time we have taken inspiration from many animals, like birds to flight or fish to dive, and we have created technology to try to replicate it.

And of course, this means that we may even be able to extend or improve a given physical task, subtasks, or action.

Robotics is all about:

Sensors + Actuators + "Inter-Hardware" + Computing.

If you remember from the first chapter in our brain (computing here) we have 3 main types of neurons that connect and resemble perfectly this, "Sensory Neurons", "Motor Neurons" & "Interneurons", so it is no coincidence that we go the same way when we develop robotic solutions.

Besides the challenges derived from building physical devices, the hardest part comes when we try to give "life" to them, or make them act or react to any situation, especially the ones not foreseen at design time.

For that we need to **add a layer of intelligence** to it, mostly using algorithms, from simple sets of rules to fully-fledged neural artificial networks that try to mimic, somehow, what we "think" a physical brain does.

So, it is not enough to build a robot o automate a task, we need to include the algorithms to perform the task, subtask or action.

And to train these algorithms we will need also data, and depending again on the task, subtask or action, the data gathering can be a hard challenge.

It is true that we already have algorithms that match and surpass human intelligence in several domains, but they do it at the expense of huge quantities of labeled data (mostly done by humans at the moment), and usually at great expense in computation costs.

The real challenge of the new Artificial Intelligence algorithms that we are building is to learn with "few" data points, more less like a small human child, that can learn incredible things, some of them almost effortless, without the need of huge amounts of trails and errors.

So, to sum up in your quest to find the right tool to automate a physical task three factors are needed:

Robotics + Algorithms + Data

If your task does not involve the physical world, the last two factors will still be needed and are explored next.

Digital Tools

Automation can lead to radical new ways to perform a task, but it is usually a good strategy to try to replicate or mimic what we humans already do first, since we already tend to optimize what we do once we are masters of anything.

I defined 3 levels of automation capabilities, so you can easily map them and measure the impact of several digital tools in the automation journey.

Level 1: "Basic" Automation features.

Level 2: Intermediate Automation features.

Level 3: Advanced Automation features.

Level 1: "Basic" Automation features:

Some of the existing software tools have to some extent ways to automate embedded in them, so a first approach will be to look there, to see If there is something already built in, to help you.

One option is that they have included some settings for **"batch" processing or "macro" recording or automated actions** per se, where you can set a few parameters and it will process underneath everything for you.

For example, imagine that you work in a creative agency, and daily you work with 100s of images, and one action that you repeat a lot, is changing the resolution of the images, if you use Photoshop[49], a widely popular photo editing tool, you can record an "action" using the action window, do the resolution change for a single image, then you can use "Automate" menu to create a batch process and repeat what you recorded with a folder full of images.

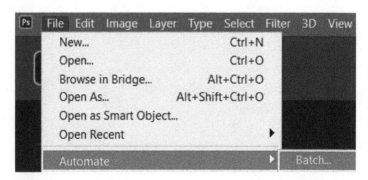

Other option to look for is the availability of a "**scripting language**" in the software you are using.

It is true that it will involve some basic notions of coding, something that may seem too far away for some people, but my view, is that **we all need to learn the basics of programing**, you don't need to be an expert in the field but at least know the basics.

Once of the factors that have helped me automate over the last 30+ years is precisely my coding skills, I learnt my first programming language (Assembly[50]), with 8 years, won my first contest a few years later, and have coded in more than 20 languages, still code regularly and never stopped since my early self-employee days, to being CEO of several startups to leading big teams, I think it is a fundamental need at all possible roles and layers in any organization and even at the personal level.

If over the last century, learning a second or even more "human" language was fundamental for many reasons, now learning at least one computer language is paramount, since the closer we get to how technology works the best will be our understanding of it.

In fact, I think that **oversimplifying the use of technology, will increase the gap between humans and machines**, unless you foster your literacy about how it works, and learning to code is a great way to narrow this gap.

Depending on how close they are to the innerworkings of computer chips, programming languages are divided into:

Machine Code[51]: basically, they are bits and bytes, as instructions to make the electronics of the computer chips work, without any further "translation" or compilation, all the other languages, to be executed, need to be converted onto this. Worth noticing that programmers do not usually create directly machine code, in most of the situations, besides for example hardware drivers programming and other tuning scenarios.

A example of machine is code is the following:

```
4d 5a 90 00 03 00 00 00 04 00 00 00 ff ff 00 00 b8 00
00 00 00 00 00 00 40 00 00 00 00 00 00 00 00 00 00 00
00 00 00 00 00 00 00 00 00 00 00 00 00 00 00 00 00 00
00 00 00 00 00 00 18 01 00 00 0e 1f ba 0e 00 b4 09 cd
21 b8 01 4c cd 21 54 68 69 73 20 70 72 6f 67 72 61 6d
```

The numbers and letters you see above, (hexadecimal numbers) are the first few instructions of machine code from the Microsoft Word[52] software I am using to write this book. Is beyond the scope of the book to explain it, but as you can see it is not easy to understand by humans.

And usually this machine code varies between different computer chips and architectures.

Assembly: a low-level language, closest to machine code, but with a small level of abstraction to make it readable to trained humans, it is in the group of second generation computer languages, it needs to be compiled into machine code to be executed. Nowadays, like machine code it is not used by programmers besides a few scenarios where code optimization is critical.

For example:

```
mov    eax, 3
mov    ebx, 5
add    eax, ebx
```

The previous instructions are needed to add up the numbers 3 + 5, "mov" and "add" are instructions and "eax" and "ebx" are something called registries in some computer chips.

High Level compiled languages, like C[53], C++[54], Basic[55], Pascal[56], C#[57] or Java[58] to name a few, where the abstraction goes deeper, they are easier to read and code, while keeping most of its capabilities. Also, the compiler creates at the end a machine executable code, so the source not is not exposed to someone just executing it, only to the programmer who code it.

A example source code could be:

```
public class AutomateOrBeAutomated {
    public static void main(String[] args) {
        System.out.println("Hello World!!!");
    }
}
```

The above Java code lines will show, once compiled, the phrase : "Hello World!!!" , first defining an "object" or "class" named "AutomateOrBeAutomated", that includes a function "main" where the execution starts and where another function is called "println" to print the line of text.

Still not easy to understand, if you know nothing about it, but much closer to human language than machine code.

Scripting languages[59], also high level, with the main difference that they are compiled or translated to machine code in real time, under the hood, instead of being the end product a executable file, so you are always sharing the source code, with its advantages and disadvantages.

But they are in general, easier to learn and a great a minimum way for all to get more out of technology when we need it. If you have never coded a good start could be the **Python**[60] language widely popular nowadays, even thought to kids at some schools.

For example:

print("Hello World!!!")

With the above Python code line, once executed, will also show, the phrase: "Hello World!!!" without the ", as you can see simpler than the other languages explored so far.

There are many other scripting programming languages like JavaScript[61], VBScript[62], Perl[63], or AppleScript[64] to name a few, and they also enable many possible automation scenarios, since most of them can be integrated with a wide variety of third-party apps. But also, many software suites already have its own scripting language or a variant of the above to automate.

Many vendors use them usually in its desktop apps like:

Most Microsoft[65] apps like the Office suite or its
operating systems.
Most Google[66] apps.
Many Apple[67] Mac OS X apps.
Most SAP[68] apps.
Most Adobe[69] apps.
Most Autodesk[70] apps.
Most Oracle[71] apps.
Many ERP & CRM vendors like SAP or Salesforce[72].
Many operating systems based on UNIX[73].

To name just a few, but it is easy that most of the
desktop apps you use regularly are scripting enabled,
some may even come with a software development kit
or SDK[74] including several Application Programming
Interfaces or APIs[75] to code the different functionalities
they provide.

Just type in a web search engine the name of your app
followed by " API" or " SDK" or " Scripting", for
example "excel API". There are usually many tutorials
and books already written with guides of these
scripting languages for specific software applications.

Level 2: Intermediate Automation features:

Another option when your app doesn't allow scripting or basic macro automation, or if you want to go to a deeper level of automation, is trying to hack it at the user interface level, using for example some of the existing **RPA[76] or Robotic Process Automation tools**.

Oversimplifying a lot, you can think of them as "macros" on steroids, the idea behind it, is to record all the interactions and inputs you perform in your computer when you are doing something, and then, over a set of possible scenarios, repeat them automatically for you, only when some given conditions are met.

The inputs to replicate and automate can be mouse movements, screen taps, clicks, keystrokes, data coming from the network and so on, and they are usually repeated over a given time flow of events.

Some of them can go even further and do for example pattern recognition in images and videos or semantic analysis on texts to trigger one or other action. The idea is to mimic what a human will do at each point in the execution time through one or more apps.

Some of the companies and software tools in this field are:

Automation Anywhere[77]   Blue Prism[78]   UiPath[79]

Automation Edge[80]   Workfusion[81]   Another Monday[82]

All these are commercial tools, have a set of common features with more less subtle differences, a few unique capabilities and some have specific solutions for industries like for human resources, finance, insurance, supply chain, customer service, telecom, energy, health care or for the public sector to name a few.

It is a good approach to take a look at them before starting your automation journey since some solutions could save you a lot of time, but beware that they are usually not cheap, but some have a "free" very limited plan, anyway is good to review them first before getting into building your own solution.

They usually come with several tools to design your automation workflow, like this one from BluePrism:

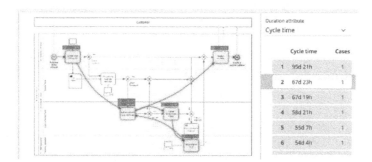

And tools to deal with many activities, like this one from the user interface of UiPath Studio:

Other option instead of using commercial software is using an open source one, as a start point to develop your own, or as the final solution, if it covers your needs, the truth is that there are not many open source solutions in the field of RPA yet, but expect more to come soon.

For windows one option is OpenRPA[83] a project started by *Allan Zimmermann*[84], still it is early days but worth watching it's progress, and for some scenarios maybe a valid option to try, https://openrpa.openrpa.dk/

Another popular digital tool in the automation toolbox lately, are the Chatbots[85], where you build a digital agent that mimic some of the behavior you will have in a given conversation with another human, they usually involve the training over a given corpus of data, where you cover all the frequent steps of a conversation about a topic.

Besides choosing the right technology, the data you need to train it, is usually the hardest part to get, and the critical factor determining the success of failure of an initiative in the chatbot space.

There are several solutions from companies like Microsoft Azure Bot Service[86], Google Dialog Flow[87], Amazon Lex[88] or IBM Watson Assistant[89], and many others that are domain specific.

Google Duplex[90] for example goes a step further enabling the chatbot not only to interact with humans but to trigger its start and hold a more complex conversation to some extent as a first prototype of a concierge for you.

And there are many other sector specific tools, for example this one to deal with scheduling x.AI https://x.ai/ and help you coordinate calendars and meetings.

x.AI[91]

Or Emma https://emma.ai a travel assistant (when travel gets to normal after Covid-19) that helps you also with scheduling related tasks.

emma.ai[92]

It is not easy to be updated in this field since every time there are more apps to cover some sectors or applications, and the landscape is growing quickly, some keep in business for long, some die quickly, but beware of the "AI" hype word, that sadly is becoming overused for products or services and by companies that don't really do any state of the art AI at all.

Level 3: Advanced Automation features:

The next step will be to fully integrate and use the current machine learning capabilities and algorithms or even develop new ones tailored to your use case.

In that regard to automate any digital task, subtask or action, before the machine could learn how to automate it, we need to gather data of how it is performed.

Essentially you need to create a labeled dataset, usually containing a timeline of events that build the actions you want to replicate and automate.

It is not uncommon to see a link between the digital and the physical world for hybrid tasks.

For example, if we are using hardware sensors too, you could already have the source of data to start with, embedded in them. The key point here is integrating the two worlds using a circular approach between then:

Gather Data from the Physical World (**Sensors**) > Compute it in the digital world (**Algorithms**) > Get back to the Physical World, interact (**Actuators**) and gather data again.

Most Sensors and actuators come with a software development kit or SDK including several Application Programming Interfaces or APIs to handle them at low level, sorry again for the acronyms but this world is full of them, unless you are a coder, something by the way, as we discuss earlier, we all should be, at least a minimum level.

If not, you will need to rely on someone to help you with this task, maybe while you learn or another possible option is to use some visual apps for the basics, some are built by the manufacturers of sensors and actuators or by a third party, they will usually do not involve coding, but will limit the capabilities to what is already pre-defined by the developer.

If on the contrary it is a fully digital task, the data gathering should be easier, as long as you are the one creating it or controlling its flow, otherwise you will need to obtain first access to the data that describes your tasks, subtasks or actions, with some restrictions or regulations that, by the way, usually vary in different countries or regions.

The idea is that at the end you should have data to train a model, once the model is ready the next phase will be deploying it and feeding it with the real time data you want to automate, and its outputs should help you automate the decisions you need to take, the simplified scheme is as follows:

Gather Training Data > Model Training > Model Ready > Deploy Model > Real time Data > Automated Decisions > And Back to Improve Model Constantly

If the data changes over time, and it usually does, the model should be re-trained periodically to keep it updated to the variations in time of the data. So, this is usually a circular approach again and not linear.

To explore this scheme, once you have gathered the training data, one option will be to use existing machine learning algorithms provided as services to train the model that will understand them. There are many use cases where we already have trained algorithms and models for some scenarios, others you will need to provide your data first to re-train or tune the existing model.

The main cloud providers, like Amazon, Google, Microsoft, IBM and other vendors, already have tools and prebuilt existing models for most of the following scenarios:

For Natural Language Processing:

Insights and relationships from unstructured text.
Document exploration & Analysis.
Translation.
Transcription, Speech to text or text to Speech.
Sentiment Analysis.

For Visual Recognition:

Object detection in images and videos.
Action detection.
Face recognition.

For Other scenarios like:

Recommender Systems.
Forecasting.
Fraud Analysis.

An interesting case is emotion recognition through visual recognition and speech analytics, with one of the pioneer figures in the field *Rana el Kaliouby*[93] with her startup <u>Affectiva</u>:

Affectiva Inc[94]

And of course, there are hundreds of startups working on specific applications for almost any industry like: Advertising, Education, Healthcare, Transportation, Finance, Real Estate, Insurance, Industrial, Retail, Agriculture and many others.

You can find a good and updated selection of most of them at the yearly *Matt Turck*[95] Data & AI Landscape <u>https://mattturck.com/data2019/</u>

This is the last edition of his landscape, check his website since maybe after the release of this book a new one is available.

Another interesting resource are the research studies from CBInsights, this is for example the last one about the "top" 100 Artificial Intelligence startups from 2020 in many sectors.

CBInsights AI 100[96]

If your use case is totally new, you will need to build you own algorithms, or hire someone to do it, in my previous book **From Big Data to Artificial Intelligence**[97] I cover the basics if you want to know more, and it contains resources to kickstart your journey into the A.I. world, and that is by the way, one of my main activities, to help companies of all sizes to implement real A.I. in its cores, so stay in touch if you want my help.

Making money with automation

One of the questions, that many people ask me, is the following: But if I teach machines to do my job, I will be irrelevant and will be replaced, what is the point of participating in the process? And worst if I work for someone else, they will benefit from it and not me.

It is true that **if you still work for someone else, sooner or later your job will be performed by a machine**, but maybe, depending on your age and role, you will be able to avoid it, and retire before that happens.

If not or even so, being part of the automation of your job may help you extend the time you keep the job, and in that regard keep the income flow.

If you have an active role in the automation of your company, basically you can make yourself more relevant, and more importantly leave your mark in the future Artificial Intelligence that will replace what you do, sooner or later, and if you are part of it, your experience will be somehow represented.

And for all age groups the good strategy is mixing the above with an active learning of the tools and tricks of automation.

The new reality is that due to the Covid-19 outbreak in 2020, the world is moving very fast to a complete readjustment of "Globalization" or even "De-globalization" due to getting back to produce locally and work from home, but also triggering a developing turmoil in many sectors from travel to real estate. Since we are in the verge of a true and massive "work from home" scenario, that will probably last beyond this crisis, and all the "non-physical automation", can be done mostly "at home", it is clearly one of the best options if you need to make a change in your career.

And currently there is a shortage of qualified professionals in the field of Automation and Artificial Intelligence, so focusing and re-skilling on it can payoff.

It is again true that eventually the demand will drop as machines replace also these tasks, but until then, my view is that is better to be part of the movement than left apart.

If you are concerned about the implications of a jobless society it is a topic covered in the following chapter.

As long as we can, it is better to surf the wave instead of being carried away by it.

Let's explore possible revenues from automation at the personal and professional levels.

Personal level:

1.- By **monetizing your data**, It is still an emerging trend, but it is true that you should own the data you produce, and it will be fair that anyone who uses it and profits from it, shares proportionally the profits with you and all the other producers of data, but with the rooted startups that rule the digital world, it is still close to an utopia to think that they will change their business models to take this into account.

But even so, this does not stop other innovative entrepreneurs like *Dana Budzyn*[98] & *Shane Green*[99] cofounders of a startup called UBDI https://www.ubdi.com/

UBDI Inc[100]

UBDI is the acronym of Universal Basic Data Income, to do something close what the name implies, with your permission they link your social network accounts like Facebook, Twitter, Instagram, Pinterest and others and apps like Spotify or Fitbit and others, and basically generate a user profile with your data, and offer you to use it in paid participation market research studies and other initiatives.

At the time of this writing they operate only in the US but exploring its deployment in other countries.

Initiatives like this are a great first step in the right direction, until a true **ownership, sharing on your premises and monetization** (if desired) is really achieved for all the data that you produce in any digital device.

2.- By being able **to keep your job** for longer, since it is the only real alternative if you want to be competitive, business as usual in almost any field, is not an option if you want to keep your job.

it is true that some jobs will be simply, fully replaced very soon by machines, and if you are in one of them the best approach is to re-skill as soon as possible, and make a change in this direction, and at the same time helping to automate your current job, instead of only attaching to it, while it last, or even worst trying to delay or sabotage it. If you are in that position, my advice will be to use your last steps there, to help, take advantage of the situation and use it to learn some of the automation tricks.

The first jobs to be replaced, will be the easier to automate, in fact you can use my **Automatability Score Formula** explained on chapter one to find how easy your job will be automated, instead of the task, subtask or action point of view, just ask the same question but for your job as a whole, if it is too abstract select the main tasks you perform and start there. The higher the automatability score the higher risk to be replaced.

It is hard to create a comprehensive list of jobs in risk of automation. But many institutions and researchers have explored this, like the pioneer 2013 research from Oxford Martin School of Economics[101] "The Future of Employment: How Susceptible Are Jobs to Computerisation?" by *Carl Benedikt Frey*[102] & *Michael Osborne*[103]

Oxford Report[104]

Or the 2018 study from OECD[105] "Automation, skills use and training" by *Ljubica Nedelkoska*[106] & *Glenda Quintini*[107]

OECD Report[108]

Or the 2019 World Bank[109] Report "The Changing Nature of Work"

World Bank Report[110]

I think that you should use them a first approach to the subject, and not as a sure to be fulfilled premonition, since for example, even two jobs with the same title, can have very different automatability scores with the formula I described. So, it is better to explore it deeper instead of getting carried away by each new report that pops up.

Most of these reports, "predict" that the jobs with the highest chance of automation are drivers, accountants, paralegals, cashiers, line cooks, financial analysts or telemarketers to name a few.

With this said, it is true that some reports can help you raise the awareness needed, but it is good to explore it yourself, with your own data and characteristics.

Remember it is a mix of many factors, like the **readiness of the technology to automate**, the **availability of the data**, the **cost involved,** the local and global **regulations** that could delay it, the **repetitiveness of the task** and the easiness to translate it to **algorithmic** terms.

Even if the timespan to its automation looks far away in time, it is a good advice to re-check this every few months, since what is hard to achieve today maybe easier tomorrow, and in a dynamic world doesn't make much sense to use static measures to take decisions, or take them and never revisit.

Anyway if you are an active part of the automation of your job, think that the way you worked will somehow live on, since the algorithms and possible robots that will replace you there, will have "your essence" too in its core, and more importantly it will help your transition to new or remaining roles in your organization (or in others), since you will be demonstrating continuous value creation to your employer and skills valued by others.

It is quite challenging to predict the future, and probably we will never have enough data to do it, but some jobs are already being replaced by machines, some will be in less than 5 years, and probably most of them in less than 20. Anyway, this is not at all a forecast but a tendency at the beginning of 2020, it is key to keep being updated so you can see it evolve and act upon.

Have in mind that one of the impacts of the Covid-19 outbreak will probably be to speed up this process, we are already seeing for example automated robots used to deliver goods, medicines and food in this crisis. But anyway, it is hard to predict the reach and how long will it last, at least at the time this was written.

3.- By **getting yourself on the field**. A very interesting approach, and great follow up or complement to the previous approach, good if you are employed at the moment, or the best possible path if you are not employed.

There are many new jobs being created, some existing ones are being upgraded, and many new ones will appear as technology advances.

Besides the jobs explored in previous chapters, some others are:

Data Analyst: Dealing with data gathering and processing.

Data Scientist: Building algorithms to understand the data.

Data Engineer: Setting up the technical infrastructure for the data to flow.

Computer Vision Engineer: Using algorithms to make sense of visual data.

Machine Learning Engineer: Using tools to deploy machine learning models.

Roboticist: To build robots.

Research Engineer: To build new science.

Principal Scientist: To lead the development of new science in your field.

Analytics/Machine Learning Director: To lead teams.

Several project management related roles along these lines are other possible jobs.

Becoming an Investor in Artificial Intelligence, Machine Learning, Automation and Robotics startups is another way too.

There are also platforms where you can participate in several microtasks like the Amazon Mechanical Turk.

Mechanical Turk[111]

But have in mind that the tasks here are usually data processing and the wages are at the lower side of the spectrum.

Business/Organization level:

1.- By optimizing your **business model** or finding new ones, there are plenty of business models, either for companies or for nonprofits, some still work, some worked and some never worked, but the truth is that theory almost never stand up without tuning in the real world. Anyway, Business Schools, Scholars, VCs and a few consultants, do excruciating studies of the most successful companies to extract the pure gold, that is the business model/s they use to thrive.

Contrary to common sense the best ones, are very simple in essence, but hard to put to practice, since reducing a full company success into a few words, a single model canvas, or a few slides, could be a masterpiece of synthesis but putting it to work in the real life, is always tricky since life, again, is not static, but quite dynamic, and people, markets or societies tend to change, sometimes faster than we expect. That is why **most of the new business models are dynamic too**.

The critical point when introducing Automation and Artificial Intelligence, is precisely being open, if needed, to change from end to end the business as usual way of doing things in your organization. Sometimes it will only enhance the existing business model, but sooner or later it will probably imply a radical change in it.

In a non-automated business model, you could rely heavily on workforce or third-party providers to perform it, once automated this should shift to computation and machines.

For example, the travel (now travel-tech) industry has seen this, first hand, since the end of the last century, from plenty of people doing the paperwork of reservations, tickets and alike, at physical travel agencies, now almost nonexistent, to a self-service, internet enabled, user centric web aggregators, where machines underneath do all the transactions, at the beginning of the century.

But did this end there? No, it kept evolving nowadays with automated recommender systems A.I. based, chatbots as the customer service, and starting to include also virtual and augment reality experiences for "remote travel", maybe one of the hot topics once the Covid-19 outbreak is under control and the travel industry recovers somehow, or even if the outbreak lasts.

Some common, key aspects I will recommend fostering and having in mind for these new business models are that they need to be: **Automated, user driven, fully personalized** and focused on **scalability at computational (not human) cost**.

2.- By **reducing costs** and improving competitiveness, linked to the previous one, a bit oversimplified the role of the CEO has been always two-fold, increase turnover and reduce cost, and automation and Artificial Intelligence are the critical tools to achieve it.

If you automate, you reduce the time and resources to perform any task so inherently as long as your automation costs are controlled, you will reduce the cost for your organization, and therefore you will reduce time to perform them and in the process you will increase the competitiveness too.

I am asked by CEOs of big corporations if automation can reduce their workforce 10 fold or 100 fold, and the truth is than with a timespan of 5 or more years for most of the sectors of activity it could, and since it may look dramatic, and it will be for many people due to the layoffs, it is also true that a new startup with 10s of employees already, could also end replacing a stablished big corporation with 1000s of employees.

So on this front, it is the moment to think how to handle the remaining human employment to cope with this new era, and regulators must play an active part on it, there is no consensus yet on how to change the model, but one of the options is reducing progressively the working hours but maintaining more less the wages, so more people can still be employed while automation takes over. An open question for all to solve together.

3.- By Getting **more insights & "intelligence"** of your activities, once you start including a data layer in any organization, and once you start also trying to understand it, insights start to pop up too. Analytics is the art of making meaningful questions to data, also not a new science, but a first critical step in the right direction.

But Analytics per se, does not pay off, unless you start to take actions, but even traditional analytics techniques are a good first step, but not enough to tackle some of the current business challenges, mainly due to the exponential increase in volume, diversity and speed of the data generated.

An Automation processes usually also include a radical increase in the amount of data flowing at any organization, which is a good thing, since more data if understood will mean more tools to impact for good the activities of any corporation.

So, it is a virtuous circle, **data > insights > automation > data > insights**..., a loop that "never" ends, that keeps feeding from the products of the automation processes we perform.

Analytics is not out of fashion per se, but it is true that it is being replaced in many situations by Artificial intelligence algorithms that go beyond what was possible a just few years ago, and now Automation is simply the way to go.

4.- By providing **new products or services** enabled or discovered by Artificial Intelligence. Yes it is the time to rethink what your company or organization does, and include in your value proposition **Artificial Intelligence driven products and/or services**, not because it is a new fancy trend, but because it is your responsibility to provide your clients, users or stakeholders with the best solutions to their needs, and that's more than probably better resolved by using A.I.

It is also the time to explore how A.I could help you do that, the first step will be to think of, what I call the **"impossible" factors**, or the things that you would have loved to add to your products or services and you never did because at the time when you tried, they were "impossible" to implement, due to factors like: not enough resources of any kind, non-existing enabling technologies, negative market conditions or lack of support from stakeholders, to name a few.

Now it is the time to **rethink again** these "crazy" things that seemed impossible in the past, but **with the lenses of Automation and Artificial Intelligence**, to see if now they are enabled by it, and start to be possible, not just because you could now, but because if you don't do it and keep business as usual, someone will do it and replace you very soon.

CHAPTER THREE:

Automate My Society

The end of Democracy?

For centuries, humans have tried to live in societies, with some success and with some notable failures, the idea of having a set of rules for all to follow, with rights and responsibilities, is in itself the root of living without getting into the ancient art of war.

Here is where the invention of democracy, in its many current arguably shades, from capitalist based to socialist, looked like the final trend in a set of government models tried through history.

Democracy may not be the best government model, and probably needed still a lot of iterations to get better and avoid many of the pitfalls it has since its inception, but nevertheless it has enabled somehow long peace and prosperity periods for many countries.

One of the fundaments of democracy, and of other government models too, is the role of the leader and representatives, elected somehow, from the population at large.

These **politicians have the responsibility to take the best decisions to make the country and its inhabitants prosperous and provide the basics**, so they can start and keep a life worth living. If corruption, extreme bureaucracy and bad long-term planning doesn't ruin it in the process.

It is also common to divide the government into several departments or ministries, that are supposed to match the development and areas of interest in any given country, like education, healthcare, employment, energy, commerce, housing, defense and so on. Most of these departments are very much the same in all countries, maybe with a few differences to reflect the singularities or priorities of each one. The first country to name a Ministry of Artificial Intelligence[112] was the United Arab Emirates in 2017, and at the time of this writing it was the only one, I am wondering what at are all the other countries waiting to have one?

Besides the "supreme" leader, usually the president, each of these departments hold a top minister or secretary to rule the day to day basics of its area, taking the fundamental decisions to run the country, with the help of a congress, usually a senate too, and supported by a set of civil servants or public officials that range from thousands to millions, depending on the country at hand.

In summary, a sometimes quite big, network of people and assets, elaborating and enforcing rules and taking decisions for the country to operate, in some countries it could be up to 30% of the total employment on the upper side and about 6% in the country with the lowest number.

But wait, **can't we foresee a future where all the decisions are taken by a machine instead of a human?** Couldn't we train an algorithm with the best proven set of actions from the past? So, in theory, it will be able to decide the best moves in each of the areas a government should address.

May look farfetched, and the truth is that still it is, since we lack still of some critical factors to achieve it, just a few initiatives in this regard have been tried, being the first a robot in the city of Tama in Japan by *Michihito Matsuda*[113], that ran for mayor, ending third.

The biggest issue, besides public support, is **how are we going to train, these "robotic" leaders and civil servants, and avoid the usual biases that come from our human nature?**

To train an algorithm you need data, and there is where the challenge resides, finding and curating good data related to how to rule a country so a machine can learn from it.

Also, the number of variables involved are huge, many are just unknown or potentially unmeasurable and probably many of them influence critically the outcome of a given political decision.

The changes through time in the social structure can also have a fundamental impact in the outcomes and it is possible that decisions from the past could not reflect correctly the decisions to take in the future giving new circumstances. Also, the amount of possible data to use is a big challenge in terms of volume and acquisition.

This should not stop us to purse this avenue, or at least lay the foundations before it is too late, **if we embrace our limitations and failures**, that looking to the past are many, **we could be able to overcome them**.

Machines are starting to be better than us, in just a few narrow scenarios, but sooner or later they will surpass our human capabilities in all facets, or what some call Superintelligence[114] like the great author *Nick*

Bostrom[115] and others Singularity[116], my view is that no matter how hard we try to avoid it or even to control it, will be futile. The only theoretical possibility I see is a global coordinated ban of all technology so it doesn't keep getting better, almost impossible to fulfill and anyway with other very undesirable consequences attached, like the impossibility to feed the almost 8 billion people living on planet earth, If you ban the use of technology altogether.

Another undesirable scenario, that may slow down or stop Superintelligence, is a cataclysm of biblical proportions happening on planet earth, maybe due to our lack of vision to take care of it, or by nature uncontrolled future events. And I don't think **the Covid-19 outbreak** is going to be it, on the contrary it **will speed up the adoption of technology** and digitization of societies, for example like working or learning from home.

So, my point of view is that we should influence for good as much as we can, and while we can, the future developments of machine intelligence, since this is our current responsibility, since probably we will be the last un-augmented humans in the loop.

We don't know in advance, and I think is even out of our reach, how in the future "intelligent" machines, when the Superintelligence point is reached, will "rule" the world, and probably, besides as building a theoretical scenario or as a science fiction exercise, it is a waste of time and resources to get carried away by it, but we should not discourage to think or theorize about of it.

But on our current reality, **we do know most of the failures of our current government systems**. My open question will be: **Shouldn't we start doing something about it?**

And the answer for me is yes, and that is why I think we should start including machines in the loop, but doing all we can to include everyone and don't leave anyone out in the data we use to train them and avoiding the known biases.

One approach could be to start building what I call **"simulated government environments"**, mirroring the existing ones, where we can start creating these artificial intelligence systems to take simulated decisions on full autonomy, so we can contrast the outcomes of real and virtual environments.

This is similar to the approach when we build algorithms and **split data**, so we can train models, learning with older data to predict the future, for example using all the data we have let's say from a given sector from the years 2000 to 2020, what we do is use a subset of the data, we take only data from 2000 to 2018 to "predict" the data that we already have from 2019 to date. This way you can check the predicting performance of your model, with data that you already have.

These simulated environments should be feed with real time data, and a good idea will be to start with areas where we already have the data and the past decisions, and probably the least critical ones, so once we move it to the real world, we can still learn and tune, minimizing the impact of failures.

What is key is to create them with full autonomy otherwise we will be adding more human biases.

In fact, this is the big question at large, when we create automated decision systems, how to avoid the possible biases due to human factors, either in the design of the algorithms or the data pipelines.

If an automated government will mean the end of democracy as we know it, is something still in the realm of thought, but it should not stop us to explore it. One possible option is that it finds a better way to rule beyond democracy or it could be embedded inside it, if it learns from the best use cases of governments. Time will tell and better if we act now.

The new rules

Do we need to invent new rules to cope up with the coming change?

The short answer is yes, we could think that having machines doing the jobs of politicians and bureaucrats is enough.

But the problem comes, when the outcome is to perpetuate the existing flaws of a system that was not invented to be automated.

If we get rid of the biases that come with the approach to learn from an existing set of actions and goals, and instead we approach it as a **paradigm shift**. Then maybe we could end with new models that **solve issues instead of perpetuating them**.

This in itself is great challenge, since so far the only way we know how to teach (humans or machines) is trough examples and experience, but if the examples are flawed or there are hidden biases, we could not guarantee its effectiveness, and could end up with augmented or new unresolved problems.

Basically, each country uses a set of rules as the basics for its governance, most with a "constitution" or something like it, It is commonly agreed that the first approach to this was the "Magna Carta[117]" by King John of England[118] in 1215.

This constitution is usually approved by an entity like a parliamentary system, more less in its current form started a millennia ago, being the first probably in

Iceland, and a bit later and the first in Europe, in the city where I was born León[119] (Spain) the "cradle of parliamentarism"[120] in 1188 by Alfonso IX[121] King of León at that time.

But being the rules dictated by a supreme ruler o by the represented citizens, the truth is that most of the countries includes a set of rights and responsibilities, enforced by plenty legislations and legal documents, in theory covering the basic relationships between its inhabitants to take care of things like the ownerships of land and goods or the mechanisms of trade to name a few.

Are these "old" rules still valid in today's terms? Are they advancing at the pace our technological society is? The truth is that probably not, even without taking into account the automated world we are headed, just with the implications of the evermore digital world, in general they are not moving at the same speed as our society moves.

Some because they are **overregulating** and probably slowing the needed development and the good outcomes that can come from it, and in the other side by keeping older outdated legislations in place, that leave a lot of aspects **underregulated**.

When selecting the rules for an Automated society instead of just using the previous base of knowledge, we could mix with it or replace it with **machine "creativity" to go beyond the previous experiences**, so far there has been a lot of great successes of creative algorithms, mostly what we call Generative Adversarial Networks[122] or GANs for short pioneered by the great Artificial Intelligence researcher *Ian J. Goodfellow*[123] and others.

In other settings, a variant of this technique is behind for example the "next" Rembrandt[124] created by an A.I. or the team behind "finishing" the Beethoven's unfinished tenth symphony lead by Matthias Roeder[125].

The rules that we need to foster in a new society are a bit different from the ones we may found in the artistic domain, but **maybe, using this artificial creativity, we will be able to create new models of governments to test, also in a simulated environment first**, that may include new rules to live by.

If you wonder why I decided to include this chapter about our Society and the next about our World, is because even if they are mostly in the realm of thought, I think it is the time to start thinking about them, so once they shift to the realm of possibility we have at least to theoretical foundations or a few practical tests done to start with.

Thrive and the quest for competitiveness

We are entering an era where we all could thrive and have a prosperous life due to the new paradigms of automation that will lead to radical changes in the way we generate our income to live, at least in theory, **at a fully automated society there will be no need to compete to thrive**.

But **until we get there, in fact the opposite is true**, the countries that get there faster will have the leverage and advantage.

So, unless at a country level, a good automation strategy is undertaken, the most probable outcome will be a rapid reduction in GDP[126] (Gross Domestic Product), way beyond what the Covid-19 outbreak is doing, and in the midterm a critical impact in the wellbeing of its inhabitants.

Through history we have plenty of examples of empires that rise and fall, or economies that flourish and perish sometimes at an incredible speed. If you think it trough, it is something that seems inevitable to stop, at least with limited resources and if you what to include all the inhabitants of planet earth.

At a fully automated society the resources won't be infinite, but they could be optimized to a level where we can get rid of many of the imbalances we see in our current world.

The resource allocation could perfectly match the needs at any given point in time, and act accordingly to the events that can impact it, like production changes due to seasons, natural events and alike.

If we ever reach that point, will mean, that we had enough intelligence or had outsourced it to machines to solve the critical and new paradigm of population growth, before it is too late.

Meanwhile our competitive nature will probably drive us to the other side of the spectrum where **the quest for competitiveness can exacerbate the existing inequalities of our world, and/or create new ones**.

In this sense the challenge is to keep the right balance between the need to compete to thrive while we build the foundations for a future where the competition is no longer needed. Any of the two approaches alone will lead to catastrophic outcomes, since if we focus only in competitiveness at all cost, most of the world we be left apart, and we can't focus only on building the new future until the time is right, since there is a subtle reality, we can't stop the current world and then re-start it, or maybe we can to some degree? since the Covid-19 outbreak is showing us otherwise.

The transition won't be easy since we will need to shift towards a new world almost taken from the utopias imagined by *Plato* thousands of years ago or by the philosophers and science fiction writers of our time.

All countries should have a clear Artificial Intelligence and Automation strategy, and create at its core competencies to be creators of the technology, not just mere users, remember the wrong and harmful view in the long term is thinking that A.I. is just another tool, and so they think there is no problem in buying it and not getting involved in its development.

It is good to have commoditized A.I. for some well know use cases, and even so, we must question if the datasets used to train the models, really are representative, or we need to use others that reflect better our realities.

From a country standpoint it also means, that the public entities should lay the foundations and pave the way so private entities and individuals can get involved in developing the use cases for Automation and Artificial Intelligence, being guarantors of its safe and unbiased use, but not overregulating it, killing its possibility to grow and compete.

The sad news is that most countries are not having the right approach towards Artificial Intelligence and Automation, for most is almost not existent, drawing a terrifying landscape in terms of competitiveness and in the long-term wellbeing of its inhabitants.

It is so sad, that at the beginning of 2020 just a few countries have a consistent and well-funded Artificial Intelligence Strategy with enough resources to make the country thrive, for that I think that there are three key ingredients:

1.- Having a great pool of **talented individuals & entrepreneurs** that are continuously updated. My diagnostics is that most countries don't have enough, but the good news is that most of them could reskill and train.

2.- Having enough **technical resources and computing capabilities**, and most countries sadly rely on others, they can rent it or buy it, but they don't produce it.

3.- **Investing** a huge amount of is GDPs and having a consistent long-term **strategy** in this field. My terrible diagnostic is that less than 10 countries in the world more less have it, being the critical factor driving the un-competitiveness of many countries in the mid long term.

Maybe it is not too late for all the countries, but if you identify yours is not doing enough in all of these three areas **is the time to advocate for it, before it is too late,** since we all will feel and suffer the devastating effects of business as usual or just doing nothing to fix it as soon as possible.

Moral compass & Automation for Good

Differentiate between what is good and evil is something can we teach a machine to do?

Can we create a training set of examples that are not biased? Can we even agree with a universal definition?

One of the main fears that we humans have in regard of machines taking over, is the possibility of our own extinction due to killer robots deciding that they are better off without us.

And to mitigate it, some think that we can make robots obey the famous three laws of robotics[127] by *Isaac Asimov*[128], or maybe we can create the also famous red button[129] for Artificial Intelligence, to stop all this at our will.

My view is that neither of these options seems feasible in the long term, since what we are creating, is something that will surpass our own, great but limited intelligence, so trying to outthink them doesn't seem plausible to me. Should you trust my view about this?, I think that it is always better for everyone to build an informed opinion, mine beyond traying to philosophize and thinking ahead about the subject, it is based on being in the trenches of researching it, and building Artificial Intelligence algorithms for many years, and also seeing it's progress over the last 30 years.

This is my opinion, and take it as such, **basically with our un-augmented fantastic but limited biology we cannot compete or evolve at the speed machine intelligence will.**

It is like trying to make a worm outsmart a human, sorry for the comparison, but in terms of intelligence, if we don't do something else, sooner or later we will be the worm in this example. So, our capacity to compete with machines will be limited by our biology, unless we are able, and agree to, augment ourselves with technology too.

Anyway, whether we reach and live that point in time or not, the best approach, at the moment, is trying to **teach machines to be as fair as possible, even if it means to go against our sometimes biased and selfish nature.**

This is another challenge to overcome in the automation journey, and another justification to involve everyone in it, so no one is left behind.

Some may think that will be better if some people are not included, since they have proved to be harmful for our societies, and this could be a wise option, or we could leave the Artificial Intelligence to compensate for it, a philosophical debate that may take place in the future and another open question.

The more problematic usages of Artificial Intelligence so far, are the ones related to altering the continuous learning data or the learning procedures to create bad or tampered outcomes.

This has been used to exploit for example the learning architecture of a chatbot teaching it to be racist, or fooling the vision systems at some self-driving cars to fool them and miss identify a real stop sign as a fooled 60 miles per hour one, or to generate fake audio or video of people and use them for monetary scams, misinformation or to manipulate opinion to name just a few.

This is a growing concern, and over the last few years, at all the Artificial Intelligence international conferences I attend, is a recurring growing topic, from tens of papers presented on the subject to thousands, **fairness in machine learning is not just a trend, but an exponential growing concern in the field**.

So when you build your automated systems is something to have in mind too, since automating almost always involves taking real time decisions, and one of the sources of the problem is the new data that is used, if it has not been anticipated in training, and could be exploited to find flaws in the design of an algorithm.

Since **most of the current machine learning algorithms are "black boxes"** due to the humongous number of parameters and layers involved, there is huge difficulty, to say the least, for us humans to understand them.

It is critical to tap into the things that we can control, like for example the data we use to train them, this is easier when you build your own models, if you use third party trained ones it gets more complex, sometimes almost impossible to trace how and with what data it learned in the first place.

So, using your own data and building and training your own algorithms is the way to reduce or at least try to control most of the factors related to algorithm fairness.

If we have the right moral compass it could permeate to the automated machines we will build for any purpose, but if we are not an active part of the process, we will need to trust what others do, and for something as critical as the future of humanity **I don't think it should be left only to technologist and entrepreneurs to decide what is good or wrong.**

One of the latest attempts to think and foster global good strategies for all is the so-called SDGs or Sustainable Development Goals by the United Nations:

SDGs[130]

This 17 Goals, No Poverty, No Hunger, Good Health, Quality Education, Gender Equality, Clean Water and Sanitation, Renewable Energy, Good Jobs and Economic Growth , Innovation and Infrastructure, Reduce Inequalities, Sustainable Cities and Communities, Responsible Consumption, Climate Action, Life Bellow Water, Life on Land, Justice and Peace and Partnerships for the Goals, looks like a great framework to start with, and why not have them in mind when we decide to automate.

The main event where the implications of Artificial Intelligence with this framework is at the core context of it, is the AI for Good Global Summit organized by the ITU[131], International Telecommunication Union, the XPrize Foundation[132], most of the United Nations entities and a few other partners.

AI4Good[133]

It is a yearly event in Geneve[134], Switzerland where 1000s of participants from almost 100 countries gather to explore, discuss and connect problem owners with problems solvers, and one of the few conferences I usually attend, in fact **the premier presentation of this book was going to be there in May of 2020**, but due to the Covid-19 outbreak the event was postponed, like almost all the events in the world.

Anyway if you want to learn more about the topic of "Automation for Good", I truly recommend you to go through the recorded sessions from past years and if possible attend one in the future, glad to meet you there.

CHAPTER FOUR:

Automate My World

The end of countries?

The idea may seem farfetched, since from very early on we humans have tried to build clans and tribes that later (oversimplifying a few steps) become countries as we know them today.

And the sense of belonging to any of them is usually, if not taken to the extremes, a feeling that empowers and have helped in the past to achieve common goals.

Through history one of these countries has become the main superpower or the empire that somehow ruled the most of the world of its time or at least a big part of it in square miles, like for example: Romans[135], Mongols[136], Umayyads[137], Chinese[138], Russians[139], Spaniards[140], British[141] or Americans[142] to name a few.

But at a regional level many other countries have also ruled or still somehow rule its area of influence.

The truth is that during some periods of time these global leaders have provided peace and prosperity, for many, but history goes that it was preceded and/or lead to periods of fight and war to achieve or keep the power, some even say that all generations through history have lived or will live a war, but I think is a hard to prove statement, unless your relax the definition of war.

But, what if there is a method to get rid of the need to have countries?

One of the beautiful side products of space exploration is our ability to see our planet from out there, with the eyes of others, and thanks to technology, unless you are one of the privileged less than 500 people (cosmonauts, astronauts or taikonauts) that have flown to space in human history. They usually describe it as **the overview effect**[143], since there are no country boundaries only natural ones.

Will it even be possible to have no countries?

If we take only into account the whereabouts of humans over the last few millennia or some of the flaws and pitfalls that we tend to gravitate towards, like envy, greed or avarice, the short answer will be no.

But if we let the darkest parts of our human nature, or the events that activate them to be ruled by an artificial intelligence that is built to avoid or override them, it could be possible.

This means that we will need to limit our freedom to achieve these, in principle, honorable goals? Well the short answer is yes.

But if we think it through, it is something we already do to live in the countries where we inhabit, with the rules that we agree to live upon, so having our freedom conditioned is the price we already pay to keep our way of life to some extent.

If you lived lately in one of the many countries where the Covid-19 outbreak lead to limits in the freedom of movement, you may have experienced this first hand, how for a greater good, we even enforce new rules and most of us needed to change our habits willingly or not.

Just for this last pandemic, imagine if instead of having 200 countries taking decisions, some maybe late or some maybe biased, you have only one with the global goal of having better off all its inhabitants, probably the outcome will be much different than out current reality, in terms of what it matters and is irreversible, the number of human lives sadly lost.

The resource allocation and the task assignment if though globally will be much different, than the one we have currently, country by country, even now that we already have some "global" entities to help with the process, but without any real authority, the impact is very limited.

Having this unique view of our planet, it is again something not easy to achieve, even it is difficult to imagine giving the conflicting history of many countries, but maybe one day it could be enabled by an Automated Artificial Intelligence system. And **in theory it could lead to a better world, as long as all of us, and all of our best intents are reflected in a global governing artificial intelligence entity**.

Once we have completed the automation of our own activities and of the rules that drive our societies, the next logical step will be to delegate also the global governance to it.

May also seem too trusty to say the least, and currently the technologies we have developed are not yet ready to something even close to this.

But it is also true that in the past we have done small steps in this direction, using technology for example to augment our decision-making capabilities.

The key is that once the technology is ready, we will be better off, if we also delegate the governance to smarter systems.

It does not mean that the key aspects that make us humans will fade of, in fact if the systems, that will replace the governance, learn from all, it will include theses aspects in its core, they will endure and outlive us. If so, we will be creating what I call the **Automated Global Governance Entity.**

Nature and A.I.

Can also nature be automated? Not exactly but we can take better care of it, if we convert all the behaviors of animals, plants and the full natural system to data, with something like a worldwide "**nature data layer**".

This way we could monitor and understand how it behaves and from there, have automated systems to keep it and make it thrive too.

We are starting to see the impact of the so-called Internet of things or IOT[144], even at the time I was writing this book we already have in the world three times more objects connected to the internet than humans alive.

And many studies foresee that we will have between 50 to 100 billion connected devices by 2025. To understand the full implications of these connected devices, they can have sensors and actuators of many kinds, like the ones we described in previous chapters. It is true that most of them will be in cities, but just imagine the possibilities of having them in the wild nature too, and through them monitor and manipulate for good, the environment they are located in.

We are starting to deploy incredible capabilities in remote sensing, to grasp the health and whereabouts of our planet through satellites and other imaging technics, we already have for example forests with sensors on some trees that report its conditions creating a mesh of connected entities.

It is not only about gathering data, but also starting to understand it and creating a model of the systems, regardless of what it is, could be a forest, a sea, a river, a mountain or the crops in a field to name a few, in fact **a model of everything** will draw many more insights than having the limited view of a single domain.

This way we can predict the long-term interactions that take place and shape it, and why not, improve it to the limits of the existing technology at each point in time.

It is true that so far, we don't have enough computing capabilities to truly understand and predict some complex events like climate interactions, storms, long term wind patterns, earthquakes, or many other planet scale events, it is true also that every year our capacity to understand them is expanded, even if it is just a little bit.

But until our algorithms are better at this task and our computation devices improve, it is critical to start gathering as much data as we can and don't forget to keep improving the resolution of these captures.

These two things are very relevant, **measuring is a fundamental** piece in understanding, some events simply fade in time, and we will lose track of them if they are not captured.

Most of our planet history and the whereabouts of the creatures that inhabited it is lost in time, only a few of them remain as scars in it, or can be inferred with some techniques, just imagine the possibilities if we have a real record of everything.

But also, the **capture resolution is critical**, if we again take a look back to our science history it is easy to spot several radical breakthroughs that were enabled by increasing the resolution of our measurements. For example, thanks to better telescopes we understand our place in the universe or thanks to better microscopes we saved many lives. Factors like speed of capture and our storage capacity should be considered too.

By the way, the animal kingdom is also not to be forgotten, from the wilderness to domestic animals, in a world, where in some countries there are more pets than children, something that reflects a probably disturbing trend in terms of societal changes.

Motorola[145] was the first to produce commercially, a few years ago, the first "smartphone" for dogs, and my bet is that sometime soon, we will have artificial intelligence algorithms to translate for example barks into "words". Maybe some will be surprised of what pets think of their owners once we have the technology to "translate" it.

Also their behavior and wellbeing could be improved by factors of magnitude, we are starting to see sensors attached to animals, mostly to track their location and a few biometric signals, and even so they are helping a lot in tracking health related issues, a discipline still in its infancy but with a lot to be done

So yes, **if we have data and algorithms to understand our nature world, we can take better care of it.** And if we want to go beyond that, we could start automating the procedures to handle it, in all its realms.

Automated farms for example are not any more in the realm of science fiction, in fact agriculture is one of sectors where automation played a critical role in reducing the number of people working in the primary sector and moving them to others, from ancient techniques to fully automated farms with robots and sensor all around.

There are several initiatives in this direction being one of the pioneers in the field is *Brandon Alexander*[146] with his Startup Iron Ox.

Iron Ox[147]

With the dramatic increase in population over the last century, even if we want it or not, our only option maybe going automated if we want to feed the world.

Beyond our world

I have to admit that the so called next frontier, or space has captivated my imagination since a very early age, with 8 years I was building mockup rockets fueled by fireworks on a stick, and many years later, created in 2005 a startup to explore the applications of Nanotechnology to Space Exploration.

Space has been the playground for automation for a very long time, from the first autonomous satellites that started monitoring our planet from above to the global positioning ones and many others in multiple domains from security to communications.

Beyond our planet we have sent autonomous or semi-autonomous robots to the realms of our solar system, many of them are still operating, some others reached its end of "life" for diverse reasons, and a few never made it to its destination.

Most of the advancements and discoveries in the field of space exploration over the last 60 years won't be possible if we rule out the existence of autonomous robotic machines either to reach places we still can't or to do things we still can't do.

Even in these days, where it seems that the human space exploration is closer than ever before, the use of autonomous systems is still on the rise.

In fact, due to our biological constrains we will be most likely in clear disadvantage, unless we augment ourselves, and even so for many reasons, robotic devices will be prominent in space too.

Space should be a human realm, and I expect that we will become a space faring society over the next couple of decades, but we have to solve many problems like the effects of long term absence of gravity or the increased exposure to radiation harmful to our biology or the psychological implications of long travel distances, some even will be one-way only. Anyway, I don't think any of these issues can't be solved in the future with the right technology.

Meanwhile planet Mars for example it is only inhabited by robots, until (or unless) life is discovered there or we colonize it.

Some people think that we should not explore space while we have a lot of unresolved problems down on planet earth, but I think that the opposite is true, most of the advances and discoveries derived from the space exploration have ended helping to solve problems here too, it is said for example that for every dollar spent on NASA it added more than $8 to the US Economy, and I think they come up short with this number.

So yes, **we should keep going to space and automating its exploration, to learn more about us and about our planet, to embrace our never-ending curious minds, and to enable human space travel once and of all.**

Afterword

There are moments in time when you realize that you need to change, now these moments look like are the everyday norm, and this feeling is right, we cannot stop the pace of change of our world.

We have the privilege to live what I call fascinating but defiant times in human history, where the actions we do today will have a profound impact in the future of everything.

Automation is just a fundamental need for all and every one of us, we will not survive economically and thrive as a society if don't embrace it, business as usual will lead to undesired but on the other hand foreseen catastrophic consequences, so it is the time to act and contribute to build this new world where we all could be better off.

There will be challenges to overcome, but with the mindset of lifelong learning, a helpful nature and with enough openness to keep changing at a faster pace, we could resolve them and build a fascinating future for all humanity.

We must not leave anyone behind, probably is one of the more repeated phrases in this book, and change while we can our societies and economic models to reflect the coming Automated world, and for that we need to rethink how to redistribute the resources and the roles that everyone of us will play in it.

Please do not believe those who say that Artificial Intelligence is just another technology or tool, it goes way beyond that or those who say that we will always control it and it will only be our cognitive enhancement, or those who say that it is just the fourth industrial revolution, because it will go also way beyond that, but you do not have to believe me either, keep learning, get involved, and decide for yourself if this is just a fancy trend or something else that will change everything.

Meanwhile, just in case, Automate before it is too late, and you are Automated.

Thanks for buying this book and for your time to read my thoughts and advices, and I sincerely hope it sparks the needed call to action so we all become makers and not mere spectators of the change that will permeate to all corners of our realities.

If this book inspired you, use it to inspire others, share your thoughts online, and feel free to reach me at vivancos@vivancos.com

Acknowledgments

This book in the end is the result of more than 30 years of relentless curiosity, curiosity to be at the edge of what is possible, and using or creating technology for trying to achieve it.

This would not be possible if I weren't been raised in a loving family that supported and kickstarted the spark to do it, from my brilliant father *Michael Angel Vivancos*, whom sadly passed away when I was 15, but not before he shared with me his values & attitude like hard work, be the best and do well to others, he was also a pioneer of his time at the telecom industry in Europe, also always learning, and always trying to provide not only the theoretical framework, but the tools to test them, like making the effort to provide our family with one of the first personal computers in the 80s where I learned to code and started to build the foundations of my technical acumen, systems that I used to build my first automation routines for example. And my mother *Pilar Cerezo* whom imprints in us a powerful creative mindset of an artist, with the need to continuously explore and with the endless positivity view that everything is possible with the right attitude. And thanks to my loving and supportive brothers and sisters, Michael, Anthony, Paul, Mariela, Pilar, Gabriel and Raphael. I am the last sibling of 8, and being the last has the tremendous advantage to learn from their successes and mistakes, the latter is a hard thing to do, since it requires a great deal of humility, not always easy to achieve, and patience on the other side.

Thanks also to my brother in law *Joseph M. Foces*, also a pioneer of his age, and one of the leading experts in computer networks and connectivity nowadays, whom also shared with me, to play with, the first phosphorite monochrome computer terminals in the 80s where I saw for the first time the concept of "Automated Agents", he also give away to me one of the first books about the C programming language by *Brian Kernighan* and *Dennis Ritchie*, and with whom I also traveled for the first time to Silicon Valley in the 90s to an "Embedded Systems" conference in Palo Alto.

Thanks also to my good friend and partner in my first few companies *Jesus Alido*, a pioneer artist and researcher that one day broke all his pencils to create only electronic and XR Art, a field he helped to born, with innovative installations all around the world and in also in cyberspace. He shared also a relentless curious and artistic mind, mixing art, technology and science in a perfect mix. With whom I a created in the 90s one the first internet companies in Spain doing then what we call today "digitization", and with whom I also cocreated the first virtual reality and cyberspace lab. He is also the author of the fantastic artwork cover of this book.

Thanks to 100+ startups, public institutions, universities and fortune 500s that have trusted me since 1995 in Europe and the US, to help them in the automation of their business or the development of their personal through keynote lectures, automation seminars, courses, workshops and advisory services.

Thanks to all that have let me help them in the realms of Data Science, Artificial Intelligence and Automation, and sorry in advance since I will name just a few like: *Tan Lee* and *Geoff Mackellar* at Emotiv Inc the pioneer startup in Brain Computer Interfaces, or *Miguel Machado* and *Xavi Cortadellas* at TheKeenFolks[148] the bold creative agency that solves the Digital Gap Management or *Sixto Arias*[149] at CapaBall[150] the lifelong learning company based on Artificial Intelligence.

Thanks to the groups of interdisciplinary minds where I belong, and where we share a common goal of making the world a better place, like the _IP Group (Internet Pioneers / Interesting People / Iberian Peninsula) now with almost to 2000 interdisciplinary members in 5 continents, founded by *Andreu Vea*[151], a group where many of the discussions about the world to come are explored.

Or the Co-inspiration Group founded by my good friend Joseph Picó[152] pioneer in the intersection of architecture and education, and transforming the education spaces for good, because the group mixes the right combination of technology and humanistic view of the world to come, with great minds like: *Jimmy Pons*[153], *Javier Martin*[154], *Jesus Alonso*[155], *Oscar Abellón*[156], *Consuelo Verdu*[157], *Concha Crespo*[158], *Monica Quintana*[159], *David Alayon*[160], *Fidel Rodriguez-Batalla*[161], *Curro Ortega*[162], *Felix Lopez, Sixto Arias* or *Balwinder Singh Powar*[163] to name just a few.

To *Carlos Rebate*[164] for interviewing me about Artificial Intelligence in his last book "The Antidote", Raquel Roca[165] for her interview in her last book "Silver Surfers", *Fran G. Cabello*[166] for his several radio interviews at the Human Resources Forum and *David M. Livingston*[167] for his interviews at The Space Show[168] Radio in the US.

To my good friend and partner at MindBigData[169] *Félix Cuesta*[170] brilliant mind of economics, marketing and pioneer of the virtual enterprise, author of several books on the subject with whom I share prospects and views of the automated future we will live on.

And to my bellowed wife *Rose Almarza*, not only for her continuous support but because she also provide me with her view of the humanistic side of the future to come, with fascinating and constructive discussions about this subject, and because her view of how the environment, the spaces we inhabit influence our psychology and thus will affect our automation endeavors.

I did not want to end the acknowledgments without mentioning *Fred Werner*[171] and *Juan De Joya*[172] from the United Nations, International Telecommunications Union ITU, host and producer of AI4Good, the leading event in Artificial Intelligence for the advance in the SDGs and for making the world ready for the Automated world we are heading towards. For their support, since I was going to do the premier presentation of this book in the 2020s edition of AI4Good in Geneve, Switzerland, in May of 2020, one of the many events postponed due to Covid-19 outbreak.

Lastly my thoughts and deep condolences to the families and friends of everyone that passed away due to the Covid-19 outbreak, a very sad huge loss in great minds mostly elderly all around the world.

References

[1] Jesus Alido, Electronic & XR Art Pioneer and Researcher
https://alido-com.webnode.es [jesus_alido@yahoo.es]

[2] Hippocrates, Greek physician
https://en.wikipedia.org/wiki/Hippocrates

[3] Plato, Athenian philosopher
https://en.wikipedia.org/wiki/Plato

[4] Leonardo Da Vinci, Italian polymath
https://en.wikipedia.org/wiki/Leonardo_da_Vinci

[5] Archangelo Piccolomini, Italian anatomist
https://en.wikipedia.org/wiki/Archangelo_Piccolomini

[6] René Descartes, French philosopher and scientist
https://en.wikipedia.org/wiki/Ren%C3%A9_Descartes

[7] Thomas Willis, English doctor
https://en.wikipedia.org/wiki/Thomas_Willis

[8] Raymond Vieussens, French anatomist
https://en.wikipedia.org/wiki/Raymond_Vieussens

[9] Humphrey Ridley, British physician
https://en.wikipedia.org/wiki/Humphrey_Ridley

[10] Pierre Paul Broca, French physician
https://en.wikipedia.org/wiki/Paul_Broca

[11] Santiago Ramon y Cajal, Spanish neuroscientist and pathologist,
Nobel prize winner and Pioneer of NeuroScience
https://en.wikipedia.org/wiki/Santiago_Ram%C3%B3n_y_Cajal
https://www.linkedin.com/pulse/20141026194333-13297760-a-tribute-to-the-father-of-neuroscience/

[12] Cecile Vogt-Mugnier, French neurologist
https://en.wikipedia.org/wiki/C%C3%A9cile_Vogt-Mugnier

[13] Hans Berger, German psychiatrist. inventor of electroencephalography (EEG) for recording "brain waves".
https://en.wikipedia.org/wiki/Hans_Berger

[14] Rafael Yuste Spanish neurobiologist, BRAIN Initiative leader
https://en.wikipedia.org/wiki/Rafael_Yuste

[15] Jack L. Gallant, Cognitive Neuroscientist
https://psychology.berkeley.edu/people/jack-l-gallant
https://gallantlab.org/

[16] Antonio Damasio, Portuguese-American neuroscientist
https://en.wikipedia.org/wiki/Antonio_Damasio

[17] Miguel Nicolelis, Brazilian scientist and Physician
https://en.wikipedia.org/wiki/Miguel_Nicolelis

[18] David Eagleman, American neuroscientist
https://en.wikipedia.org/wiki/David_Eagleman

[19] Mary Lou Jepsen, American Neuroscience Polymath
https://www.maryloujepsen.com/
https://www.openwater.cc/

[20] Adam Gazzally, American neuroscientist
https://gazzaley.com/
https://neuroscape.ucsf.edu/

[21] Tan Le, Vietnamese-Australian innovator and entrepreneur, Consumer EEG pioneer, Emotiv Inc CEO
https://en.wikipedia.org/wiki/Tan_Le

[22] Emotiv Inc, Pioneer brain wear startup
https://www.emotiv.com/

[23] Stanley Yang, NeuroSky Inc CEO
https://www.crunchbase.com/person/stanley-yang

[24] NeuroSky Inc, mind wearable biosensor startup
http://neurosky.com/

[25] Ariel Garten, Canadian artist, scientist, Interaxon Inc founder
https://en.wikipedia.org/wiki/Ariel_Garten

[26] Derek Luke, Interaxon Inc CEO & President
https://www.linkedin.com/in/derekluke/

[27] Interaxon Inc, Brain sensing Startup
https://choosemuse.com/

[28] Ramses Alcaide, Neuroscientist, CEO of Neurable Inc.
https://www.linkedin.com/in/pharoramses/

[29] Neurable Inc, Brain Computer Interfaces + VR Startup
https://www.neurable.com/

[30] Bryan Johnson, American entrepreneur CEO of Kernel Inc,
https://bryanjohnson.co/

[31] Kernel Inc, Neuroscience Startup
https://www.kernel.co/

[32] Elon Musk, Lifelong Entrepreneur and Visionary
https://en.wikipedia.org/wiki/Elon_Musk

[33] NeuraLink, Brain Implantable Upgrades Startup
https://www.neuralink.com/

[34] Norbert Wiener, Swedish-American mathematician
https://en.wikipedia.org/wiki/Norbert_Wiener

[35] Simplemind software
https://simplemind.eu/

[36] Clive Humby British mathematician and entrepreneur
https://en.wikipedia.org/wiki/Clive_Humby

[37] Human Microbiome
https://en.wikipedia.org/wiki/Human_microbiome

[38] Juan Enriquez, Mexican-American businessman & speaker
https://en.wikipedia.org/wiki/Juan_Enr%C3%ADquez

[39] Juan Enriquez TED Talk
https://www.ted.com/talks/juan_enriquez_your_online_life_permanent_as_a_tattoo

[40] Simon Sinek American/British author
https://simonsinek.com/

[41] Boston Dynamics
https://www.bostondynamics.com/

[42] Agility Robotics
https://www.agilityrobotics.com/
[43] Robonaut
https://robonaut.jsc.nasa.gov/

[44] Fedor Robot
http://en.roscosmos.ru/20854/

[45] HaptX haptic globes
https://haptx.com/

[46] SynTouch
https://syntouchinc.com/

[47] Shadow Robot Company
https://www.shadowrobot.com/

[48] Biomimetics
https://en.wikipedia.org/wiki/Biomimetics

[49] Photoshop
https://www.adobe.com/products/photoshop.html

[50] Assembly programming language
https://en.wikipedia.org/wiki/Assembly_language

[51] Machine Code
https://en.wikipedia.org/wiki/Machine_code

[52] Microsoft Word
https://products.office.com/en-us/word

[53] C programing language
https://en.wikipedia.org/wiki/C_(programming_language)

[54] C++ programing language
https://en.wikipedia.org/wiki/C%2B%2B

[55] Basic programing language
https://en.wikipedia.org/wiki/BASIC

[56] Pascal programing language
https://en.wikipedia.org/wiki/Pascal_(programming_language)

[57] C# programing language
https://en.wikipedia.org/wiki/C_Sharp_(programming_language)

[58] Java programing language
https://en.wikipedia.org/wiki/Java_(programming_language)

[59] Scripting languages
https://en.wikipedia.org/wiki/Scripting_language

[60] Python programing language
https://en.wikipedia.org/wiki/Python_(programming_language)

[61] JavaScript programing language
https://en.wikipedia.org/wiki/JavaScript

[62] VBScript Microsoft Visual Basic Scripting Edition
https://en.wikipedia.org/wiki/VBScript

[63] Perl programing language
https://en.wikipedia.org/wiki/Perl

[64] AppleScript
https://en.wikipedia.org/wiki/AppleScript

[65] Microsoft
https://www.microsoft.com/

[66] Google
https://www.google.com/

[67] Apple
https://www.apple.com/

[68] SAP
https://www.sap.com/

[69] Adobe
https://www.adobe.com/

[70] Autodesk
https://www.autodesk.com/

[71] Oracle
https://www.oracle.com/

[72] Salesforce
https://www.salesforce.com/

[73] UNIX
https://en.wikipedia.org/wiki/Unix

[74] SDK Software development kit
https://en.wikipedia.org/wiki/Software_development_kit

[75] API Application programming interface
https://en.wikipedia.org/wiki/Application_programming_interface

[76] RPA Robotic Process Automation
https://en.wikipedia.org/wiki/Robotic_process_automation

[77] Automation Anywhere
https://www.automationanywhere.com/

[78] Blue Prism
https://www.blueprism.com/

[79] UiPath
https://www.uipath.com/

[80] Automation Edge
https://automationedge.com/

[81] Workfusion
https://www.workfusion.com/

[82] Another Monday
https://www.anothermonday.com/

[83] OpenRPA
https://openrpa.openrpa.dk/

[84] Allan Zimmermann
https://www.linkedin.com/in/skadefro

[85] Chatbots
https://en.wikipedia.org/wiki/Chatbot

[86] Microsoft Azure Bot Service
https://azure.microsoft.com/services/bot-service/

[87] Google Dialog Flow
https://dialogflow.com/

[88] Amazon Lex
https://aws.amazon.com/lex/

[89] IBM Watson Assistant
https://www.ibm.com/cloud/watson-assistant/

[90] Google Duplex
https://ai.googleblog.com/2018/05/duplex-ai-system-for-natural-conversation.html

[91] x.AI Meeting Scheduling
https://x.ai/

[92] emma.ai travel planning
https://emma.ai/

[93] Rana el Kaliouby, Pioneer of AI based Emotion Recognition CEO of Affectiva Inc
https://ranaelkaliouby.com/

[94] Affectiva Inc
https://www.affectiva.com/

[95] Matt Turck, VC at First Mark
https://mattturck.com/

[96] CBInsights AI 100 Report
https://www.cbinsights.com/research/artificial-intelligence-top-startups/

[97] From Big Data to Artificial Intelligence 2019 by David Vivancos
https://www.amazon.com/Big-Data-Artificial-Intelligence-2019/dp/1795094834

[98] Dana Budzyn, Co-founder and CEO at UBDI
https://www.linkedin.com/in/danabudzyn/

[99] Shane Green CEO (US) at digi.me & co-founder/chair UBDI
https://www.linkedin.com/in/rshanegreen/

[100] UBDI Inc (Universal Basic Data Income)
https://www.ubdi.com/

[101] Oxford Martin School of Economics
https://www.oxfordmartin.ox.ac.uk/

[102] Carl Benedikt Frey Swedish-German economist
https://en.wikipedia.org/wiki/Carl_Benedikt_Frey

[103] Michael Osborne, Professor of Machine Learning at University of Oxford
https://www.linkedin.com/in/michael-a-osborne-176895a4/

[104] Oxford Report: The Future of Employment: How Susceptible Are Jobs to Computerisation?
https://www.oxfordmartin.ox.ac.uk/downloads/academic/future-of-employment.pdf

[105] OECD Organisation for Economic Co-operation and development
https://www.oecd.org/

[106] Ljubica Nedelkoska Post-doctoral Fellow at the Center for International Development at Harvard University
https://www.linkedin.com/in/nedelkoska/

[107] Glenda Quintini Senior Economist at OECD
https://www.linkedin.com/in/glenda-quintini-040779bb/

[108] OECD Report "Automation, skills use and training"
https://www.oecd-ilibrary.org/deliver/2e2f4eea-en.pdf?itemId=%2Fcontent%2Fpaper%2F2e2f4eea-en&mimeType=pdf

[109] World Bank
https://www.worldbank.org/

[110] World Bank Report "The Changing Nature of Work"
http://documents.worldbank.org/curated/en/816281518818814423/2019-WDR-Report.pdf

[111] Amazon Mechanical Turk
https://www.mturk.com/

[112] UAE Ministry of Artificial Intelligence
https://ai.gov.ae/

[113] Michihito Matsuda, Robot runs for Mayor at Tama
https://www.linkedin.com/in/michihito-matsuda-a7182517/

[114] Superintelligence
https://en.wikipedia.org/wiki/Superintelligence

[115] Nick Bostrom, Swedish philosopher & author
https://nickbostrom.com/

[116] Technological Singularity
https://en.wikipedia.org/wiki/Technological_singularity

[117] Magna Carta
https://en.wikipedia.org/wiki/Magna_Carta

[118] King John of England
https://en.wikipedia.org/wiki/John,_King_of_England

[119] León (Spain)
https://en.wikipedia.org/wiki/Le%C3%B3n,_Spain

[120] The Cortes of León "cradle of parliamentarism"
https://en.wikipedia.org/wiki/Cortes_of_Le%C3%B3n_of_1188

[121] Alfonso IX King of León
https://en.wikipedia.org/wiki/Alfonso_IX_of_Le%C3%B3n

[122] Generative Adversarial Networks
https://en.wikipedia.org/wiki/Generative_adversarial_network

[123] Ian J. Goodfellow Deep Learning Resercher
http://www.iangoodfellow.com/

[124] The "next" Rembrandt
https://www.nextrembrandt.com/

[125] Matthias Roeder director of Herbert von Karajan institute
http://matthias.zeitschichten.com/

[126] GDP Gross domestic product
https://en.wikipedia.org/wiki/Gross_domestic_product

[127] Three laws of robotics
https://en.wikipedia.org/wiki/Three_Laws_of_Robotics

[128] Isaac Asimov, Russian/American writer.
https://en.wikipedia.org/wiki/Isaac_Asimov

[129] Red button – The AI control problem
https://en.wikipedia.org/wiki/AI_control_problem

[130] Sustainable Development Goals
https://sustainabledevelopment.un.org/sdgs

[131] ITU, International Telecommunication Union
https://www.itu.int/

[132] XPrize Foundation
https://www.xprize.org/

[133] AI for Good Global Summit
https://aiforgood.itu.int/

[134] Geneve, Switzerland
https://en.wikipedia.org/wiki/Geneva

[135] Roman Empire
https://en.wikipedia.org/wiki/Roman_Empire

[136] Mongol Empire
https://en.wikipedia.org/wiki/Mongol_Empire

[137] Umayyad Empire
https://en.wikipedia.org/wiki/Umayyad_Caliphate

[138] Chinese Empire
https://en.wikipedia.org/wiki/History_of_China#Imperial_China

[139] Russian Empire
https://en.wikipedia.org/wiki/Russian_Empire

[140] Spanish Empire
https://en.wikipedia.org/wiki/Spanish_Empire

[141] British Empire
https://en.wikipedia.org/wiki/British_Empire

[142] The United States of America
https://en.wikipedia.org/wiki/United_States

[143] The overview effect
https://en.wikipedia.org/wiki/Overview_effect

[144] Internet of things or IOT
https://en.wikipedia.org/wiki/Internet_of_things

[145] Motorola Scoout5000
https://www.motorolastore.com/support/pet/smart-monitoring/scout-5000.html

[146] Brandon Alexander, Automated farm Pioneer CEO Iron OX
https://www.linkedin.com/in/brandonacealexander/

[147] Iron Ox Inc Robotic Farms
https://ironox.com/

[148] TheKeenFolks, Digital Gap Management
https://thekeenfolks.com/

[149] Sixto Arias
https://www.linkedin.com/in/sixto

[150] CapaBall, Life Long Learning
https://capaball.com/en/

[151] Andreu Veà
https://www.linkedin.com/in/landreu

[152] Jose Manuel Picó
https://picoj.es/

[153] Jimmy Pons
https://www.jimmypons.com/

[154] Javier Martin
https://www.linkedin.com/in/loogic/

[155] Jesus Alonso
https://jesusalonsogallo.com/

[156] Óscar Abellón
https://www.linkedin.com/in/%C3%B3scar-abell%C3%B3n-mart%C3%ADn-5a864195/

[157] Consuelo Verdu
https://www.linkedin.com/in/consueloverdu

[158] Concha Crespo
https://www.conchacrespo.com/

[159] Monica Quintana
https://monicaquintana.es/

[160] David Alayon
https://davidalayon.com/

[161] Fidel Rodriguez-Batalla
https://www.linkedin.com/in/fidelrodriguezbatalla

[162] Curro Ortega
https://singladura.net/

[163] Balwinder Singh Powar
https://www.linkedin.com/in/balvindersinghpowar

[164] Carlos Rebate
https://carlosrebate.com/

[165] Raquel Roca
https://raquelroca.com/

[166] Fran Garcia. Cabello
https://www.fororecursoshumanos.com/

[167] David M. Livingston
https://www.davidlivingston.com/

[168] The Space Show
https://www.thespaceshow.com/

[169] MindBigData
http://mindbigdata.com/

[170] Felix Cuesta
http://felixcuesta.com/

[171] Fred Werner
https://www.linkedin.com/in/fredericwerner

[172] Juan De Joya
https://www.linkedin.com/in/juandejoya/

www.ingramcontent.com/pod-product-compliance
Lightning Source LLC
LaVergne TN
LVHW041205050326
832903LV00020B/461